MW01153313

Disclaimer

The information included in this book is designed to provide helpful information on the subjects discussed. This book is not meant to be used to diagnose or treat any medical condition. For diagnosis or treatment of any medical problem, consult your own doctor. The author and publisher are not responsible for any specific health or allergy needs that may require medical supervision and are not liable for any damages or negative consequences from any application, action, treatment or preparation, to anyone reading or following the information in this book. Links may change and any references included are provided for informational purposes only.

Plant-Based Diet

200 Delicious Recipes For Vibrant Health and Radiant Energy

By Susan Hollister
Copyright © 2018

Table of Contents

CHAPTER 8: MAIN DISHES THAT EVERYONE LOVES.................................181

CHAPTER 9: DELICIOUS SNACKS AND INCREDIBLE APPETIZERS 209

CHAPTER 10: DESERTS YOU CAN FEEL GREAT ABOUT 232

CHAPTER 11: RECIPE COMPONENTS 264

CONCLUSION 314

MY OTHER BOOKS 315

Introduction

Congratulations, you have made a great decision in purchasing this book! Included are 200 delicious plant based recipes for vibrant health and radiant energy. You will also discover why a plant based diet does so many good things for you as well as how to easily implement the delicious recipes in this cookbook into your daily meals. A plant-based diet is a great way to become healthier, happier, more productive and have a lot more energy! Some of the foods included in a plant based diet are vegetables, nuts, seeds, beans, fruits, whole grains and more. Plant-based diets can be vegetarian or vegan, but they may also include certain dairy products and meat if you desire. In fact, vegetarian and vegan diets are only a couple of the many forms of plant-based diets that are popular today.

It is a proven fact that eating less meat and fewer animal-derived foods along with a plant based diet does make most people healthier and helps them to maintain a healthy weight. Plant-based diets are largely successful because they eliminate the use of processed foods that can adversely affect our bodies while fueling the body with natural and healthy foods.

Delicious Fruits and Vegetables for a Plant-based Diet

Plant-based diets tend to lower cholesterol, thus reducing the risk of cardiovascular disease. They have also been shown to lower blood pressure and minimize the risks of stroke and colorectal cancer.

A 2018 study out of the Netherlands, found that those who consumed a high rate of plant protein were less likely to develop heart disease than those who embraced a diet consisting of primarily animal protein. They also found that people who ate more plant protein, were less likely to be overweight; they didn't have to live as strict vegetarians to benefit from this diet, either. The report indicates that young and old alike can benefit from a plant-based diet, even if they still take in some animal-based protein.

The best benefit from a plant-based diet is you can usually eat as much as you want until you are full. Nothing is packed with sugars that will make you gain weight and most of what you eat is fiber rich and goes straight through the digestive system without leaving anything behind. You will fill up faster because of the fiber intake too.

One of the first things you will notice in this book is that there are no meat recipes at all. At the same time, you'll find some recipes that contain dairy products and eggs. If you have chosen to forego all animal products, you will of course be avoiding these.

I have personally had incredible results from switching to a plant based diet. I have lost weight, feel better and have a lot more energy! Are you ready to start your plant-based diet? Then keep on reading to discover a treasure trove of incredible recipes you can make for yourself, family and friends.

The Problems Of A Meaty Diet

We've all been taught that a balanced diet is necessary to sustain a healthy body. Part of that balanced diet can include eating meat. With some people, eating meat causes very real problems. In others, the *lack* of meat is potentially harmful. Your dietary needs are dictated by the unique makeup of your body. This is why you should always consult a doctor before starting a new diet.

Meat does some interesting things to your body. We have been lead to believe that meat is loaded with nutrients. However, plants tend to be a much better source of nutrients for your body.

Meat contains two primary components, protein and fat. While the protein is very good for your body, the fat is problematic. Meat tends to build up harmful substances in the body and then the body must work harder. The body bogs down and might make you feel tired and sluggish. Our digestive systems need fiber to push everything through and absorb the nutrients that it needs and purge the rest. Eating mostly meat allows the stuff we don't need to stay in our bodies longer than it should. It literally rots inside the body because it can't get out fast enough.

In addition to that problem, meat has more than its share of other issues. Unless you are eating organic meat, it probably comes from animals nourished on substandard feed. If you look out on a real farm, you will see chickens scratching in the dirt for insects and cattle eating grass in a meadow. However the sources of the meat you eat rarely get this luxury. Most likely, the animals you eat will be given prepared feed and no grass.

In addition, meat producers often inject animals with hormones, to cause them to grow bigger muscles (which make up the meat we eat). Guess what? Those hormones just don't go away once the animal is butchered. They stay in the meat that you eat. The hormones go into your body!

These animals are also given antibiotics that remain in the meat you eat. When we find humans whose bodies are resistant to antibiotics, we wonder why. There is increasing evidence that this resistance comes from eating meat containing antibiotics.

Seafood isn't immune from this problem, either. We now know that sea creatures ingest pollutants and pass them on to you.

Microscopic pieces of plastic have been found inside fish and other seafood. When you eat that piece of tilapia, you then introduce those plastic pieces into your body.

Meat is highly acidic and the human body has a difficult time breaking down acid. The kidneys can be affected by this acid. Meat is loaded with saturated fat, which our bodies also have a hard time breaking down. The saturated fat can remain in our bodies for a long time, contributing to a range of problems including heart disease, high cholesterol, high blood pressure, diabetes and obesity. Studies have concluded that a diet high in meat contributes to osteoporosis and cancer, because all that excess protein and fat accumulates in fatty deposits in the body.

Of course, you don't have to completely stop eating meat if you don't want to. If the thought of cutting out meat gives you shivers, don't do it. The basic idea behind a plant-based diet is simply to *reduce* the amount of meat you eat. Any progress in this direction can yield wonderful results, especially when done over long periods of time by making it a daily habit. You can take small steps toward a plant-based diet by gradually reducing the amount of meat you eat, replacing it with tasty alternatives. If you can reduce your meat intake to a lean hamburger, a small steak, barbequed chicken, or shrimp scampi once or twice a week, you'll be doing well.

Benefits of Plant-based Diets

Eating a plant-based diet reduces the acids you take in and increases fiber that removes wastes more quickly. When toxic wastes are removed quickly, they do not hang around in the body long enough to do harm. This can reduce the chances of developing heart disease, inflammation or diabetes. You tend to have more energy and don't get sick as often.

This diet can be adopted anytime. Even a slight shift toward a more plant-based way of eating can give you noticeable benefits. These benefits are experienced alike by the young and the old, so you have little to lose by giving it a try.

Many Choices Exist For a Plant-based Diet

Plant-based vs Vegan and Vegetarian Diets

When you ask the normal person about the differences between a plant-based diet and a vegan diet, they may say there is no difference, but there is. A plant-based diet means different things to different people; the vegan and the vegetarian diets are just two types of plant-based diet. A third is the Mediterranean diet.

You can eat meat in a plant-based diet. You just eat more plant-based foods than meat. A relative of mine adheres to the plant-based diet. Most of his meals are completely vegetarian, but two to three meals per week do contain chicken, beef and dairy products. He chooses not to eliminate animal-based foods completely and it works for him. It is hard to go completely plant-based, so allowing some animal-based foods in the diet makes it easier to sustain over time.

What to Eat

Eating plant-based foods isn't rocket science. It requires shopping in the produce section more than anywhere else in the grocery store. You can use frozen fruits and vegetables too, but stay away from produce that is processed; you'll want to avoid items like frozen green bean casserole or candied sweet potatoes. You can enjoy plenty of non-starchy vegetables like tomatoes, leafy greens, broccoli, eggplant, carrots, green and yellow beans, cucumbers, radishes and zucchini.

Eat **starchy vegetables** sparingly. You'll want to go easy on things like potatoes, sweet potatoes and other root vegetables, legumes (beans and lentils) and corn. You can enjoy all kinds of **fresh fruits**, but avoid sugar packed, highly processed juices.

Whole grains are plant-based. You can choose from oats, brown rice, quinoa, barley and the like. White bread and white rice are highly processed and therefore, should be avoided. Whole wheat pasta is better for you than regular pasta, but couscous is considered acceptable.

Nuts and seeds are used sparingly because of their fat content. Include avocados in this category. It's ok to eat nuts and seeds, just try not to overdo it.

Sweeteners contain some potential pitfalls. Most humans are addicted to sugar, but refined sugars are anathema to a plant-based diet. At the same time, artificial sweeteners contain potentially dangerous chemical compounds. Avoid anything ending in –ose and flee from high fructose corn syrup. You are much better off using plant-based sweeteners such as stevia and xylitol. Other sweeteners that can be used are honey, maple syrup and agave syrup.

Should you choose not to eliminate all **meat**, make sure to purchase lean meats, seafood and skinless chicken. Lean pieces of pork are also good. Bacon is out of bounds as are any greasy and processed meats if you are being serious about the diet.

Shopping for a Plant Based Diet

Some people who subscribe to a plant-based diet restrict themselves to organic food, but that is not necessarily essential to the diet. The only requirement is that you "cut down" on meats, eating them two to four times a week. You can eliminate meat altogether, if you choose; just ensure that your body gets enough complete protein through plant sources. But it is always a good idea to get organic products when possible.

The following suggestions will help you know what to shop for when using a plant-based diet. The list includes fresh produce and many other pantry items to keep on hand:

Fresh Fruits and Vegetables – focus mostly on leafy greens for salads and add other vegetables and fruits to create salads. Avoid starchy vegetables like corn and potatoes if you hope to lose weight and stay away from avocados if you have heart problems or want to lose weight. If you are diabetic, carefully track the amount of fruit you eat, as these can spike your sugar levels dangerously.

Nuts and Seeds – I love sunflower seeds on everything. They give just the right kind of crunch and flavor to enhance almost anything. I also love cashews, but watch how much you eat because of the high oil content. Almonds are also delicious and great for energy. Many nuts and seeds contain little oil, but they still should be eaten sparingly.
Try and avoid salted nuts and honey-roasted nuts if possible. I like to throw a tablespoon of sunflower seeds in my salads and some almonds or cashews in dishes that could use a bit of crunch.

Chia and flax seeds are high in Omega-3s, so keep them in your pantry. Flax seeds need to be ground for the digestive system to benefit from them and chia seeds should be soaked in liquid before you eat them because they can absorb 10 times their weight in liquid. It is a good idea for men to eat flax seeds sparingly. If you eat too many chia seeds dry, they can absorb the liquid in your digestive system and create problems on the other end.

Beans and Legumes – These items contain plenty of fiber and will fill you up quicker than lower fiber vegetables. They also keep you from getting hungry. I enjoy cannellini beans, pinto beans, kidney beans, great Northern beans as well as the earthy flavor of lentils. Canned beans often are laden with salt, so try to find the low salt varieties or use dried beans and wash and cook them thoroughly.

Breads and Grains – You can eat breads and grains on a plant-based diet because they come from plants. Just watch how much you eat; they can pack on the pounds. Whole grain breads are best; white bread removes the fiber so no nutrients are left. Look for the words "whole grain" on the packaging to make sure you are getting what you want. But if you are truly interested in optimizing your health, it is generally best not to eat breads and pasta very often.

Other grains you should always have on hand are quinoa, couscous, farrow, bulgur, hull-less barley and oats. Rice is an option and there are many forms from which to choose. You can use short, medium or long grain rice, including Basmati and Jasmine rice. Rice can be found in colors such as black, purple and red, but never use white rice, as it is highly processed. Choose whole grain pasta, keeping in mind that it usually needs a longer boiling time than regular pasta.

Bake with whole-wheat flour and never white. Health food stores have a variety of acceptable flours such as oat, barley, kamut and rye.

Dried Fruits – Keep a few dried strawberries, cherries, cranberries and other fruits on hand to throw into oatmeal or salads, but use them sparingly because they have concentrated amounts of sugar and can lead to weight gain. Dried fruits can give you that little touch of sweetness that we all crave. They can be stored for a long time under air-tight conditions and serve you well in the off-season.

Frozen Foods – frozen fruits are great if there is no sugar added. Frozen vegetables are also good for your plant-based diet. I like frozen vegetables better than canned because you don't get the added salt canned varieties can introduce into your diet. They also taste fresher. I also love popping frozen grapes and strawberries in the heat of summer.

Non-Dairy Milk – Some plant-based milk products include almond milk, soy and cashew milk, but keep an eye on the sugar content; it can be astronomical, especially with the flavored varieties.

Protein Powder – A good protein powder is an excellent addition to your diet. I highly recommend a "Plant Based" protein powder. There are many great choices out there. Just do your research and try and find a product made completely from plant protein. If you are active or do strength training a good protein powder shake is great to have daily. My favorite powder is Gold Standard by Optimum Nutrition. Simply add honey to your smoothie if you want it a little tastier.

Flavoring Agents – these items add a pop of savory highlights to your food. Keep them on hand to increase the flavorful attractiveness to your dishes. This category includes flavored vinegars, lemons and limes for their juice, herbs and spices (fresh is best but dried is acceptable), mustard, olives (preferably not packed in oil), reduced-sugar ketchup and the full panoply of spices, the world over. Feel free to explore different combinations and intensities; flavor experimentation is one of the lesser-known delights in life.

The next chapter introduces you to the details and will help you easily get started. Soon enough you will be cooking delicious recipes that will give you the energy you need to really perform at your best in your life!

Enjoy The Many Benefits of A Plant-based Diet

Chapter 1: An Energy Charged Lifestyle

Plant-based Smorgasbord

Plant-based eating isn't just a diet; it's a lifestyle. If you don't eat much meat to begin with, you'll have a fairly easy dietary adjustment. On the other hand, if you are accustomed to eating meat with almost every meal, you'll find it a challenge. Just start off slowly eliminating meat from your diet and do it gradually over time.

Just learning to cook plants as a main course can be a major lifestyle adjustment. I found myself wrestling mentally, trying to wrap my mind around the idea of using side dish ingredients to create a main course. I also was worried about getting enough protein.

The beauty of a plant-based diet is that it does not expect you to avoid all animal products. You can gradually phase out meat from your diet, or you can just shift the balance of your diet until you are eating more plant-based foods than meat. I still include meat, eggs and dairy products in my meal preparation, but not every day. I tend to eat plant-based lunches and I enjoy plant-based dinners about five nights a week, but I also include a few meals that contain red meat, just in case the doctor was right!

Let's talk about some of the lifestyle adjustments you may wish to adopt when moving toward a more plant-based diet.

Breakfast

Some people say breakfast is the most important meal of the day, but I am not one of them. I never feel like eating in the early a.m. However, it's important to consume at least *something* to sustain your blood sugar throughout the morning; you don't want it to bottom out around 10 a.m., leaving you struggling to stay awake! Food deprivation like this is what leads to crazy binge eating where all dietary restraints fly out the window! So, do what you can to get something inside your stomach, even if it is only a banana or a piece of bread.

If you can't stomach traditional breakfast foods early in the morning, you can explore the wonderful world of smoothies. You'll find a whole chapter of delicious beverages later on in this book that will go down easy and keep you going until noon.

I never used to eat breakfast, so this was a major lifestyle adjustment for me. However, after a few mornings of crashing and burning before noontime, I learned. Now I run out of the house with my smoothie in hand, sipping it all the way to work. That usually tides me over until lunch.

Kick Off The Day With A Colorful Smoothie

How Much Can You Eat?

Most diets are subtractive; they constantly warn dieters not to overeat. This is where I ran into trouble with my vegetarian diet. I once thought a heaping salad was way too much for me to eat, so I just picked at it. I thought that since I lost weight, I could lose even more by further cutting down on my portion sizes. This left me crabby and constantly hungry. It also left me sadly malnourished.

When you follow a plant-based diet, the quantity you eat is much greater than on an animal-based diet. If I had eaten the amounts as prescribed in my vegetarian diet, I probably would have been fine; I doubt I would have gotten sick. The trick is: plant-based foods are not as densely packed with calories as meat, so you will actually find yourself eating larger portions than usual. The rule of thumb is to eat about 2000 calories a day. You might find this difficult at first, but if you gradually increase the amount of plant-based food in your diet, you'll find that amount will be about right to both fuel your day and prevent hunger pangs.

You Won't Be Hungry

The plant-based diet is higher in fiber than most other eating lifestyles. This tends to leave you feeling fuller. Eating fibrous plants, surprisingly, can keep you feeling full longer, especially if you eat them for breakfast, lunch and dinner. If you *do* get hungry during the day, don't reach for cookies or crackers. I recommend you keep carrot and celery sticks in the refrigerator; you can eat them plain or dip them into a little hummus.

When Cravings Arise

Avoid processed foods

Occasionally I crave a potato chip. Of course, you can't eat just one, so before I know it, I've consumed the entire bag!

Potato chips are processed. We can tell this because they in no way resemble what a raw potato looks like in its natural state. They are usually fried in oils that are not at all healthy. So, despite my cravings, I have chosen to stop eating potato chips. But I still crave them.

You *will* have cravings. Fortunately, you can usually find a natural alternative that tastes good and can satisfy that craving. For example, some people turn to kale chips as a healthy alternative to potato chips. They are crunchy, they're easily made at home and they can be eaten without guilt in generous quantities.

I don't really like kale, so I tend to opt for zucchini, turnip, or beet chips. All of these are baked and delicious and can be found in some grocery stores. I'll cover how you can make them yourself in a later chapter.

If you don't have anything else on hand, you can always pull out a carrot and munch on that. It might not taste much like a chip, but it *is* crunchy.

You can treat all cravings similarly:
1. Look for a healthy alternative that may or may not be similar to what you're craving.
2. Look for something that matches the texture or the flavor you are craving.
3. Use healthy dips or coatings that add a pop of flavor or a unique texture.

Shop Purposefully

How many times have you gone to the supermarket with no list and just picked up whatever looked good? You can't really get away with that with a plant-based diet, especially when you're first starting out. Until you get used to it, I suggest you first settle on a meal menu, then make a list of the ingredients you'll need and mark off what you already have on hand. The rest you will need to buy. Eventually you'll have most of the non-perishable items on hand, so your shopping list will consist mainly of fresh foods.

The plant-based lifestyle will also affect how and where you buy food. You'll find yourself gravitating toward organic foods, partly because they just taste better. If they're too expensive in the stores, you might find yourself frequenting farmer's markets or even befriending local growers so you can get food fresh from the farm.

If you eat meat, you'll want to search out grass-fed meat sources. Since you're eating less meat, it's worth it to pay a little more to get the most flavorful cuts.

Fruits and vegetables are best found fresh, but in areas with a cold winter, this could get expensive. Many of the recipes in this book call for frozen vegetables.

I freeze some of my garden vegetables for use in the winter. I don't can them because this involves processing, which is something we're trying to avoid on this diet. In today's society we can find many fresh fruits and vegetables year round, even though they may be more expensive during the off season. Depending on your preferences, you may choose to pay more during that time, or you can easily stock up on items when they're cheaper in season and freeze them for later use.

Don't Bring It Home

If something you're craving is in the house, you *will* eat it no matter how hard you try not to. The easiest way to learn to do without the cookies, cake, chips, soda and other highly processed foods that are frowned upon in this diet is not to bring them home! If you exercise your "won't" power while you're at the grocery store, you won't need to say "no" repeatedly at home. At the same time, if you bring home plenty of plant-based foods that you can enjoy as snacks, you'll be able to silence those cravings and at the time train your body to prefer those foods instead.

All About Protein

The old saying that you just can't get enough protein without eating meat has been soundly disproven. Multiple studies, advances in our understanding of nutritional needs and a whole host of successful vegetarians (people who eat no meat and yet run marathons and perform amazing feats of strength, agility and endurance) have put to rest that fear.

At the same time, when you adopt any form of plant based diet, you enter the realm where getting enough protein can be a constant challenge. Your protein levels are worth paying attention to, especially if you're taking parts from several different plant-based diets, where individual meals are not planned out for you.

If you're wondering how much is enough, when it comes to protein, I can answer that question. **You need a half gram of protein for every pound of body weight**. In other words, if you weigh 200 pounds, you need to eat 100 grams of protein daily. This is doable without eating any meat at all, but you may find yourself staring at a lot more vegetables and fruits on your plate than you are accustomed to eating. This is one reason why vegetarians often find it necessary to include eggs, dairy, or fish in their diet.

Here are some plant-based items that will give you the most protein:

Sunflower seeds	1 cup =	32 grams
Soybeans	1 cup (cooked) =	29 grams
Almonds	1 cup =	28 grams
Lentils	1 cup (cooked) =	19 grams
Cashews	1 cup =	16 grams
Split peas	1 cup (cooked) =	16 grams
Black beans	1 cup (cooked) =	15.2 grams
Green beans	1 cup (cooked) =	9 grams
Peas	1 cup (cooked) =	8.6 grams
Spinach	1 cup (frozen) =	6 grams (cooked = 5.3)
Passion fruit	1 cup =	5.2 grams
Corn	1 cup (cooked) =	5 grams
Potato	1 cup (cooked, skin on) =	5 grams
Guava	1 cup =	4.2 grams
Avocado	1 cup = 2.9 grams 1 avocado =	4 grams)
Brussel sprouts	1 cup (cooked) =	4 grams
Broccoli	1 cup (cooked) =	3.6 grams
Sweet potato	1 cup (cooked) =	2 grams

While you probably won't be eating a cup of sunflower seeds in a single setting, even a quarter cup will give you more protein than a whole cup of corn! Seeds and nuts are some of the best, in terms of protein content.

By contrast, here are the protein amounts for animal-based products:

Swiss cheese	1 cup =	67 grams
Tuna	1 cup =	54 grams
Parmesan cheese	1 cup =	38 grams
Salmon	1 cup ((1/2 fillet) =	42 grams
Chicken breast	1 cup =	42 grams
Hamburger	1 cup (cooked) =	36 grams
Mozzarella cheese	1 cup =	36 grams
Steak	1 cup =	17 grams
Egg	1 cup =	17 grams
	1 egg =	6 grams
Yogurt (nonfat)	1 cup =	14 grams
Yogurt (whole milk)	1 cup =	8 grams
Milk	1 cup =	8 grams

If you're not getting enough protein, one of the first indicators is a loss of muscle mass. I know I can tell I need more protein in my diet when I become listless and tired for no apparent reason. I receive further confirmation when a can of tuna fairly quickly restores my energy levels. If you notice skin breakouts, delayed healing of cuts and bruises, or thinning fingernails, these are serious warnings that your protein levels are dangerously low and you need to give a major boost to your protein intake, now.

Keep On The Move

It is interesting how eating well makes you want to get up and do things. Before I adopted a healthy diet, all I wanted to do after work was come home and plop down in front of another rerun of "Gilmore Girls" on television. Now I'll change clothes and go for a walk; I'll take my neighbor's four-year-old to the playground; or I'll putter around in my garden. I just have more energy. If I were a runner I would go for a run. Since I'm not, I go hiking.

There are plenty of ways you can keep your body moving. From fidgeting to roller blading, there are options galore. Find something that suits your fancy and go for it. If you have friends who share your enjoyment for walking, include them in your daily jaunts; you'll find the time spent even more enjoyable.

Switch out activities periodically, in order to avoid boredom. This will also get a different set of muscles involved and generate fresh interest across your entire body. You can also create some variety by finding a different environment for your activities. When I hike, I usually search out a wooded trail. However, I find equal – or even greater – enjoyment at the beach. Some days I just walk around my neighborhood, while other days I'll head for a nearby park.

Eating Out

Unless you frequent fast food restaurants, an option that is verboten on this diet, you'll find plenty of places that have plant-based foods on the menu. Most restaurants are quite aware of the trend toward healthy eating. They are now offering whole foods and vegetarian options for those who want them. If you don't see anything among the main dishes that suit your dietary requirements, often the appetizers will have something you can enjoy. If not that, you can almost always find a salad on the menu. Sometimes I have found the staff quite willing to prepare a dish of steamed vegetables for me, something outside the menu. There's no harm in asking.

Getting Started

Plant A Garden To Keep Fresh Vegetables Close At Hand

The transition to eating little or no meat can be a challenge for some people. My advice is to go slow and easy. If you eat three meals a day, this means you have 21 meals to work with over the course of a week; seven breakfasts, seven lunches and seven dinners. Start out by making five of the seven breakfast meals plant-based. Unless you are used to eggs every day, that should be a snap. Smoothies are great for breakfast and they can keep you full until lunch.

I also make my own breakfast bars to take with me to work since I don't like eating early. The key here is making your own. Avoid commercially produced granola and breakfast bars; they contain way too many highly processed ingredients. However, it'll only take an hour to make your own breakfast bars out of healthy ingredients; you'll find a recipe in the breakfast chapter. That way you can use unprocessed ingredients that are packed with nutrients and you can avoid the chemical preservatives that are so prevalent in commercially prepared foods.

Make only two days of lunch entrees plant-based at first. Brown bagging your lunch can raise some challenges, but most workplaces provide at least a refrigerator and a microwave for your use. It's fairly easy to heat up leftovers from dinner the night before or choose from the cold entrees included in the lunch chapter of this book.

If you are on the go during the day and don't have time to stop for lunch, take a smoothie with you in a cold keeper bag. If you have a smoothie for lunch, you may want to eat something more substantial for breakfast. I've found that when I drink smoothies for both breakfast and lunch, I'll start craving something to chew on by mid-afternoon.

Start out with only three plant-based dinner entrees each week. In addition to the recipes in this book, you'll find plenty of plant-based and vegetarian dinner recipes on the Internet. When you're starting out, I recommend alternating meaty meals with meatless meals. You can relax on your meaty days and cook something familiar. Before long, the meatless meals will become easier to prepare, too. Then you'll feel more comfortable about substituting more meatless days if you wish.

I followed this weekly meal plan for almost a month before I started adding plant-based meals to lunch and dinner. I gradually substituted in more plant-based dishes until I reached a balance of foods I'm comfortable with. I still enjoy one or two meals each week that are full of meat and I haven't completely removed eggs or dairy products. I've just cut back on my consumption.

Supplements

Supplements Can Be a Great Addition To Your Diet

Not everyone on a plant-based diet needs supplements, but many people do. I am one of them. Over time I've discovered that my body needs a boost from supplements to keep healthy. Especially when you first start out on a plant-based diet, you might need the help of supplements to ensure you're getting the proper balanced nutrition.

Before you start on a new diet, I recommend you discuss your proposed changes with your physician. Your doctor can run periodic blood tests to catch any deficiencies before they become dangerous. Then you can alter your diet or take supplements to make up for the lack.

Here are some of the most common vitamins and mineral supplements that might be useful when you follow a plant-based diet:

Vitamin B12 – This vital nutrient is most prominent in seafood and organ meats. Since we're steering you away from meats however, the best plant-based sources of vitamin B12 are fortified cereal, fortified nutritional yeast and fortified nondairy milk. Nutritional yeast has long been a staple in vegetarian diets. Beyond these few plant-based possibilities, B12 supplements are recommended.

Vitamin D – is essential to the health of our bones and it helps regulate blood sugar and blood pressure. Vitamin D helps the body absorb calcium and phosphorous and makes the muscles, heart, thyroid, pancreas and brain function properly. It is essential for proper functioning of the immune system. It helps prevent a host of diseases, including autoimmune diseases, rheumatoid arthritis, Multiple Sclerosis, Crohn's disease, Alzheimer's and some forms of cancer.

This is one vitamin I would highly recommend you receive in supplement form, as part of your plant-based diet. Sunlight exposure has been determined an ineffective way to get enough Vitamin D. It's absorbed through the skin, but even if you run around outside in a bikini all day long, the sunlight in most places in the world won't give you enough of what your body needs to be able to create the vitamin.

It is estimated that 40% or more of the American population is deficient in vitamin D, even if they eat meat. I know I am; I've been taking supplements for years. However, you'll want to use this one under doctor's supervision; too much vitamin D can actually harm your body, so you'll want a professional to periodically check your body's vitamin D levels.

Omega-3 fatty acids – Also known as omega-3s, these are essential to your health. There are three types: ALA, EPA and DHA, hence their name. Of the three, DHA is the most critical.

DHA is present in your brain and is responsible for enabling memory, creativity, emotion, language and attention. The omega-3 trinity as a whole is integral to stabilizing heart rhythm, it is known to repress age-related mental decline and it has been shown to prevent some forms of cancer.

Plants are full of ALA, most prominently chia seeds, canola oil, walnuts, basil, hemp seeds, soy in its various forms and flax seeds. You can also find omega-3s in Brussels sprouts, fresh spinach greens, broccoli and in omega-3-enhanced eggs, laid by free-range hens whose diet includes flax seeds.

EPA and DHA are found in greatest quantities in salmon, sardines, herring, anchovies and other fatty fish, through the algae they eat. Because of the increasing levels of toxins in the ocean and consequently in its seafood, these omega-three sources are increasingly suspect. Fortunately, however, you can go directly to the source; seaweed contains huge amounts of EPA and DHA.

These are just a few supplements you may need as you transition to a plant-based diet. You are making this change in order to be healthy, so it is essential that you ensure your body receives the proper nutrition along the way. I highly recommend bringing a physician alongside to monitor your nutritional balances while you are making this adjustment.

Oddly enough, while there are a host of popular diets available that could be considered plant-based, there is no single "official" plant-based diet. The Mediterranean diet is probably the most well-known, but it seems that for each specific health need that arises, a plant-based solution appears on the scene to address it.

In the next chapter we will explore the top eight plant-based diets. I have included sample recipes to give you a feel for what to expect with each one.

Chapter 2: Recipes From The Best Plant Based Diets

A recent trend has emerged in popular diets. Each diet may vary in its details, but today we are witnessing a distinct move away from meats and toward a larger proportion of plants and veggies in our meals. In this chapter I have taken eight of the most popular diets that minimize the use of meat – if not cutting it out altogether and have described them, along with a few sample recipes for you to explore.

While I do eat a little meat, I also follow a largely plant-based diet. I borrow some recipes from the Mediterranean diet, but I mix them with dishes from the Ornish diet and basic vegan fare. In addition to descriptions, I've provided some of the plant-based recipes from each of these popular diets.

Explore Your Plant-based Diet Options

Mediterranean Diet

The Mediterranean diet is one of the most popular healthy plant-based food regimens. The countries in the Mediterranean region

– primarily Greece, Italy, Spain and France – share a culinary culture that is often considered one of the healthiest in the world. Mediterranean's gravitate toward fresh produce, plucked directly from the garden and extensive use of whole grains. They avoid highly processed items (especially sugars) and their diet is low in saturated fats. Cheese and yogurt are popular in this diet, while fish, poultry and meats are limited to a few meals a week.

The benefits of this diet are many. It lowers the risk of cardiac issues. It normalizes cholesterol levels, blood pressure and blood sugar; it may even help you lose weight.

It isn't difficult to follow when you eat out and a great deal of information is widely available online, including recipes, startup plans, sample meal plans. Ingredients are easy to find in grocery stores, farmers' markets, or in your own garden. Because you are using fewer processed foods, in other words, you're eating more fresh produce, your meals are incredibly tasty. The low-carbohydrate component promotes healthy energy levels and clear-headedness.

The Mediterranean Diet Is All About Fresh Foods

Garbanzo Bean Salad

Garbanzo beans, also known as chickpeas, are full of fiber and protein. You can find them dried like other beans, but I prefer to buy these canned. You'll just want to rinse off the starch from the canned beans before using them. This recipe yields four servings and is delightfully refreshing.

Ingredients:
1 15-ounce can garbanzo beans, drained and rinsed
1 large roma or plum tomato, seeded and diced
½ medium sized green bell pepper, seeded and diced
1 small onion, finely chopped (I like purple onion)
1 clove garlic, minced
1 tablespoon fresh parsley, chopped
1 tablespoon olive oil
1 lemon, juiced

Directions:
1. Pour the drained and rinsed garbanzo beans into a medium bowl and add the diced tomato and bell pepper.
2. Add the onion, garlic and parsley and toss.
3. In another small bowl, mix the olive oil with the lemon juice and pour this over the salad.
4. Toss well so all is coated, then cover the bowl.
5. Refrigerate for one hour before serving.

Rustic Tuscan White Bean Stew

This stew contains no meat, but it's still bulky and full of flavor. I use vegetable broth here, but if you're a carnivore you can substitute beef broth.
Yield: 6 servings

Ingredients:
1 tablespoon olive oil
2 cloves garlic, quartered
1 slice whole-grain bread, cut into half-inch cubes
2 15-ounce cans cannellini beans, drained and rinsed

½ cup water
2 more teaspoons olive oil
1 yellow onion, chopped
5 more cloves garlic, chopped
3 large carrots, tops removed, chopped into coins
1 teaspoon salt, divided
1 bay leaf
¼ teaspoon pepper
1 tablespoon fresh rosemary, chopped, for garnish
6 sprigs of rosemary, also for garnish
1½ cups vegetable stock (See recipe, Chapter 11.)

Directions:

1. Make the croutons first by swirling a tablespoon of olive oil in a skillet over medium heat.
2. Add the two quartered garlic cloves and sauté for one minute. Remove the pan from the heat and let it set for 10 minutes. This will transfer the garlic flavor into the oil. Remove and discard the garlic pieces.
3. Return the pan to the heat and stir in the bread cubes. Sauté, stirring constantly, until they are lightly browned – about four minutes. Place in a bowl and set aside.
4. Place one can of the beans in a small saucepan with a half cup of water and let it come to a boil. As soon as the liquid is boiling, remove the pan from the heat and mash with a potato masher until the beans become a paste. Set aside.
5. Add two tablespoons of olive oil to a large pot over medium heat. Sauté the onions and garlic for about two minutes before adding the carrots. Sauté for an additional two to three minutes.
6. Add the salt, bay leaf and pepper along with the tablespoon of fresh rosemary.
7. Add the mashed beans, the whole drained beans and the stock; simmer for 10 minutes or until hot.
8. Ladle the stew into bowls and top each with a sprig of rosemary before serving.

Flexitarian Diet

The Flexitarian diet is very healthy and may help you to lose weight. This diet is "flexible," meaning you can have meat and animal products part of the time. Not every day though. It also includes meat substitutes such as tofu, beans, peas, nuts and even eggs and milk to ensure that you get the proper amounts of protein.

The diet is also heavily into fruits, vegetables and whole grains. It encourages the use of herbs to add flavor and other benefits. It allows the use of natural sweeteners, including agave and honey.

Breakfasts are about 300 calories, lunch around 400 and dinner 500, giving the dieter a total of around 1500 calories per day. Of course, the actual amounts are determined by your gender, weight, height and activity level.

Flexitarian: Mix of Vegetables, Fruits, Dairy, Eggs and Meat

Most of the meals are very tasty, even the meat substitute dishes. In most cases, you will lose weight on this diet because of the portion restrictions and the types of foods you eat. Because this is a commercial diet, it can be a challenge to find recipes online, but the approved cookbook can be found at most bookstores. The diet is fairly easy to follow, as long as you count your calories.

Flexitarian Cauliflower Tacos with Crunchy Slaw

I was pleasantly surprised at how wonderful this recipe tastes. I've even prepared it several times for friends, who devoured it with unanimous exclamations of pleasure.

This recipe makes eight tacos. I've separated the ingredients into three sections: the almond preparation, the slaw and the tacos themselves. These tacos taste even better topped with crushed avocado and salsa.

Ingredients:
Almonds:
> 1 cup whole almonds, raw
> 2 tablespoons hot sauce (See recipe, Chapter 11.)
> 1 tablespoon tamari (you can use gluten-free but always use low-sodium)
> 1 tablespoon olive oil

Slaw:
> 1 cup shredded green cabbage
> 1 cup shredded red cabbage
> 1 small jicama, julienned
> ½ cup of the prepared almonds
> ½ cup cilantro, chopped
> Juice of 1 lime
> 1 teaspoon olive oil
> Pink salt and black pepper, ground – to taste

Tacos:
> ⅓ cup slivered almonds, blanched
> ½ of a large cauliflower (about 3 cups), cut into florets
> 1½ teaspoons ground cumin
> ½ teaspoon paprika
> 1 teaspoon chili powder
> ½ teaspoon red pepper flakes

½ teaspoon pink salt
¼ teaspoon garlic powder
¼ teaspoon onion powder
¼ teaspoon oregano
1 pinch black pepper
2 tablespoons olive oil
1 package 6-inch corn tortillas

Directions:
Almonds:
1. Preheat the oven to 350 degrees and line a lipped baking sheet with parchment paper.
2. Spread the almonds on the baking sheet and place in the oven for eight minutes.
3. While the almonds are cooking, take a medium bowl and combine in it the hot sauce, tamari and olive oil.
4. Remove the almonds from the oven and let them cool for five minutes. Add them to the bowl and stir to coat evenly.
5. Use a slotted spoon to remove the almonds from the bowl and spread them onto the previously used baking sheet.
6. Bake for five to 10 minutes, stirring halfway through. Don't let them burn. Remove from oven and let them cool completely.

Slaw:
1. In a large bowl combine the cabbage, jicama, a half cup of the almonds from the first stage and the cilantro.
2. In a small bowl combine the lime juice and olive oil and pour this on top of the slaw. Add the salt and pepper and mix it with your hands until everything is coated. Store in the refrigerator until you need to use it.

Tacos:
1. Place the slivered almonds in a food processor or blender and pulse until they look like rice. Remove to a large bowl and do the same with the cauliflower florets. (Less than one cup at a time was all my food processor could handle).

2. In a small bowl mix the cumin, paprika, chili powder, red pepper flakes, salt, garlic powder, onion powder, oregano and black pepper, then set aside.
3. Pour the olive oil into a skillet over medium heat and let it warm up. Throw in a half tablespoon of the spice mixture you just made up and toast it, stirring for about 30 seconds. Add the cauliflower/almond mixture and stir to coat. Cook for five minutes or until the cauliflower is cooked through. Sprinkle a little more of the spice mixture onto the cauliflower.
4. Warm the tortillas on the stove. I use a gas stove and turn on the burner to low before laying a tortilla on the burner for about 20 seconds, flipping to warm both sides. I use tongs to remove it. You can use a skillet if you prefer. I keep the tortillas wrapped in a clean cotton dishtowel until I am finished warming them all.
5. Fill the tortillas each with about a third cup of the cauliflower/almond mixture, spooning on top some crunchy slaw. Top and eat.

Chickpea and Quinoa Burgers

This recipe uses chickpeas and quinoa to make a delicious, spicy meatless burger. This recipe makes four patties. You'll be serving them in pitas. I recommend adding greens, tomatoes, avocado and mayonnaise or yogurt to taste.

Ingredients:
½ cup white quinoa
1 cup vegetable broth
2 slices whole-wheat bread
1 14-ounce can chickpeas, drained and rinsed
1 large egg
¼ cup cilantro, chopped
1 teaspoon cumin
1 small red chili, seeded and chopped
Salt and pepper to taste
1 tablespoon vegetable oil
4 small whole-wheat pitas

Directions:

1. Place the quinoa and broth in a saucepan over high heat and let it come to a boil. Cover and reduce the heat to low. Cook for about 15 minutes or until the liquid is fully absorbed. Let it cool for about 15 minutes.
2. Place the bread in a food processor or blender and process until crumbly. Add the chickpeas, the cooked quinoa, egg, cilantro, cumin, chili, salt and pepper, pulsing until finely chopped.
3. The mixture should stick together well enough that you can shape the mixture into four patties.
4. Coat a skillet with nonstick spray and brush the patties with oil. Set the heat to medium high and cook the patties for about four minutes per side, or until brown.
5. Wrap each patty in a pita or just serve with toppings on the side.

Ornish Diet

Dean Ornish, professor of medicine at the University of California in San Francisco, published a book in 2007 entitled "The Spectrum." The book breaks down food into five categories that range from "bad" foods that you should avoid at all costs to "good" foods that you can eat more-or-less freely. Along with the food categorization, he also proposes following a lifestyle that includes exercise and strategies for stress reduction.

Most of the "bad" foods consist of meat (excepting fish), so the Ornish diet focuses on fresh fruits and vegetables along with whole grains. The diet is designed for individuals who are at high risk for heart disease. The absolute food restrictions and the exercise requirements are the main difficulties you'd encounter on this diet.

Ornish Dirty Rice and Beans

This dish is very flavorful, but it's also quite spicy. You may use regular brown rice or Basmati, my preferred choice. The recipe also calls for kidney beans, but I have successfully substituted pintos in a pinch; you just need a firm bean that will hold up well. This recipe yields six to eight servings.

Ingredients:
2 cups brown rice, dry (uncooked)
3 cloves garlic, minced
1½ cups red onion, chopped
½ cup celery, diced
1 cup carrots, diced
1 small jalapeno pepper, seeds removed and minced
1 tablespoon ground coriander
1 tablespoon ground cumin
2 teaspoons chili powder
3¾ cups vegetable stock (See recipe, Chapter 11.)
¼ teaspoon sea salt
1 28-ounce can diced tomatoes
1 bay leaf
½ cup frozen corn kernels
2 16-ounce cans of kidney beans, drained and rinsed
3 tablespoons fresh cilantro, chopped
3 tablespoons fresh parsley, chopped

Directions:
1. Preheat the oven to 350 degrees, Fahrenheit and spray a 5-quart covered casserole dish with nonstick spray. Set aside. (Note: I have also used a foil-covered 11 by 18 inch glass baking dish.)
2. In a heavy-bottomed saucepan, combine the rice, garlic, onion, celery, carrots, jalapeno, coriander, cumin and chili powder. Turn the burner on to medium high and stir this mixture constantly for four to five minutes, or until everything is lightly browned.
3. Add the vegetable stock, sea salt, undrained tomatoes and the bay leaf; stir to mix. Simmer for 15 minutes with the lid on.
4. Add the corn, drained beans, cilantro and parsley and heat through. Pour the mixture into the casserole dish, cover

and bake for 40 minutes. The liquid should absorb as the rice cooks.

Whole Grain Caramelized Onion and Spinach Quesadilla

If you like caramelized onions, you will love this dish. This recipe makes two quesadillas, so you'll have to double it for four; but you'll probably want to keep all of them to yourself. You can add non-fat shredded cheese to the quesadilla, but it really tastes fine without this nonessential addition.

Ingredients:
¼ of an onion, sliced and separated into rings
Pinch of salt
½ cup fresh spinach
½ cup cooked black beans (I warm canned beans that have been drained and rinsed)
1 whole grain tortilla

Directions:
1. Dry caramelize the onion slices by placing them in a warmed skillet over medium high heat. Sprinkle the salt on top and sauté, stirring constantly. The salt should pull the moisture out of the onions and allow them to brown.
2. Combine the spinach and black beans in a bowl and add the onions. Mix well and set aside.
3. Place a tortilla in the skillet over medium heat and put some onion, spinach and bean mixture on one side. Add cheese if you must.
4. Fold over the tortilla and toast one side, then flip it and toast the other side before serving.

Vegetarian Diet

Several types of vegetarian diets exist. While the basic vegetarian diet is purely plant-based, to make it easier to get enough protein vegetarians may also include one or more of the following in their diet:

- Eggs
- Dairy products
- Fish

Because of this flexibility, you can transition into the vegetarian diet as gradually as you wish. Over time you can reduce your food intake to two meat-based meals in a week for a while, then one and eventually cut out meat entirely, if you choose.

There is a difference between vegetarianism and being a vegan. Vegans follow a philosophy that shuns the use of anything that "has a face," using their own parlance. In addition to avoiding the meat of an animal, they avoid milk and dairy products, because consider the practice of milking to be a form of animal torture. They also stay away from eggs, because they consider egg farming animal exploitation. This philosophy extends to the boycotting of animal-based fats (e.g., fish oil) and any animal-based product, whether or not it's used for food (e.g., furs, leather).

Fortunately, whether you're totally eliminating meat from your life or just scaling back, you can now find an abundance of meat substitutes on the market today. The likelihood of losing weight on a vegetarian diet is quite high. When you stop eating meat and processed foods, it tends to reduce your caloric intake. Your diet will prove fairly simple to sustain, even when you eat out; most restaurants serve vegetarian entrees or are able to adapt their dishes to your dietary requirements.

The main challenge is to ensure that you get the right amount of protein and other nutrients that appear primarily in meats. After all, the purpose of any change in your eating habits should be driven by your desire to be healthy. That's why so many people have opted to include eggs, dairy products and/or fish in their otherwise vegetarian diet. It's less hassle. This is an easier way to ensure your diet provides the proper nutrition, while at the same time avoiding the worst of the meat-based foods.

Sample Vegetarian Ingredients

Whole Wheat Pasta with Broccoli Pesto

This dish, a lacto-vegetarian special because it includes cheese, has a fresh flavor that can't be beat. I use frozen broccoli, but you can use fresh, as long as you place the florets in boiling water for a few minutes to soften them up. The recipe yields four servings.

Ingredients:

12 ounces whole-wheat pasta (I don't usually use spaghetti, but elbows or bow ties are nice)
12 ounces frozen broccoli florets
2 cloves garlic, minced
½ cup water
3 tablespoons olive oil
½ cup fresh basil leaves
1 tablespoon lemon zest
½ teaspoon sea salt or kosher salt
2 tablespoons slivered almonds
¼ cup Parmesan cheese, grated

Directions:

1. Cook your pasta per the package instructions. After it's finished cooking, reserve a half cup of the cooking liquid before you drain the pasta.
2. While the pasta is cooking, put the broccoli, garlic and a half cup of tap water in a microwave-safe bowl. Cover it and cook on high for six minutes, stirring the contents halfway through.
3. Pour this mixture, liquid and all, into a food processor or blender. Add the oil, basil leaves, lemon zest and salt and puree until the mixture is smooth.
4. Place the drained pasta in a bowl and toss with the broccoli pesto puree. It will be dry and a little gooey so add half of the reserved liquid from the pasta and stir together. If the mixture still seems too dry, stir in more of the water, little by little, until it reaches the right consistency.
5. Divide the mixture among four plates and sprinkle with almonds and Parmesan cheese before serving.

White Bean Spinach Polenta

This dish is simply delicious. I use cannellini beans, but you can use others. You can also swap out the spinach for escarole if you like. The recipe makes four delicious servings.

Ingredients:
1 lemon
1 tablespoon olive oil
1 clove garlic, thinly sliced
1 pinch red pepper flakes
2 teaspoons fresh thyme leaves
8 cups fresh spinach
1 teaspoon kosher salt
2 15-ounce cans low sodium white beans, rinsed and drained
1 cup instant polenta (See recipe, Chapter 11.)
1 tablespoon unsalted butter or butter substitute
⅓ cup grated Parmesan cheese
1 tablespoon lemon juice

Directions:

1. With a vegetable peeler, scrape off three wide strips of lemon peel from the lemon and slice them into narrow sticks. Set aside.
2. In a Dutch oven, add the oil and let it heat up. When heated, add the garlic, red pepper flakes, thyme and lemon peel. Stir and sauté until the garlic is golden, about two minutes.
3. Add the spinach and salt; sauté until the spinach wilts, about three minutes. You will need to do this in batches, adding salt with every batch.
4. Add all the spinach to the pan and fold in the beans. Cook for three minutes.
5. Cook your polenta per the package instructions and remove from the heat. Add the butter, parmesan cheese and lemon juice and stir until the butter melts.
6. Divide the polenta evenly among four plates and spoon the bean spinach mixture over the top.

Traditional Asian Diet

People who live in Asia have lower rates of heart disease, obesity and cancer than the rest of the world; they also tend to live longer lives. That says something for their diet. The basic Asian diet is low-fat and includes rice, vegetables, fruit and fish. Asian fruits and vegetables are a little different from what you'd find in an American grocery store. They include bamboo shoots, bean sprouts, bok choy, bitter melons and taro root. An Asian market should have most of these items. Asian cooking also includes vegetables more common to Americans, such as carrots, sweet potatoes, eggplant, leeks and the like.

The Asian Diet Has Lots of Rice and Vegetables

The Asian diet is not written down and there aren't a set number of calories to be consumed in a day. It's up to you to figure out what works best for you. The good news is you will probably lose and weight and find a healthy weight realistic to maintain by eating an Asian diet.

Be careful when eating out because American Asian cuisine is quite different from the real thing. What you will find in most American restaurants is often cooked using lots of oil; it tends to include more processed, (i.e., less healthy) ingredients that are higher in calories and add toxins to your body.

The true Asian diet includes a great deal of rice and noodles, so if you don't really care for those ingredients, you might want to pass this on this one, in favor of something that better suits your tastes.

Carrot Noodles with Orange and Ginger

Carrots ARE the noodles in this dish and kids and adults alike will get a kick out of eating it. This dish is spicy and sweet, laced with orange and ginger flavors that permeate the carrots. You can use this as a side dish or as a main course. Find the fattest carrots you can find or use a spiralizer. You can serve the carrots by themselves or add some soba noodles and raisins. I also love this with a splash of Thai Peanut Sauce. This recipe serves four.

Ingredients:

6 large carrots, peeled
2 tablespoons olive oil, divided
Zest from 1 large orange, divided
1 tablespoon fresh ginger, chopped
½ teaspoon kosher or sea salt
¼ cup fresh parsley, chopped
½ teaspoon red pepper flakes

Directions:

1. Preheat the oven to 400 degrees, Fahrenheit.
2. Slice the carrots lengthwise, creating thin planks. Stack the planks and slice them carefully into sticks that are about a quarter inch thick. Arrange the sticks on a rimmed baking pan that has been covered with parchment paper. Sprinkle with a tablespoon of olive oil, half the orange zest and all of the ginger. Sprinkle on the salt and toss to coat the carrots. Spread the carrots out on the pan so that they do not overlap.
3. Place the pan in the oven and roast your carrots for 30 minutes, stirring halfway through. The carrots should be tender and lightly browned on the edges.
4. While the carrots are cooking, mix the remaining olive oil in a bowl, along with the rest of the orange zest, the parsley and red pepper flakes.
5. Remove the carrots from the oven and place on a serving plate. Pour the olive oil mixture over the top, toss to coat and serve.

Thai Peanut Stir Fry

This dish will wake up your taste buds and make 'em say "howdy." It includes sweet and spicy flavors along with a little sake, which is permitted in moderation as part of the Asian diet. Natural peanut butter or peanut butter you grind yourself is preferred, but you *can* cheat with a little commercial creamy peanut butter, if you must. This recipe yields two large servings.

Ingredients:
1 8-ounce package spaghetti, uncooked
1 tablespoon cornstarch
1 cup vegetable stock (See recipe, Chapter 11.)
⅓ cup creamy, natural peanut butter
3 tablespoons soy sauce (See recipe, Chapter 11.)
3 tablespoons honey
3 tablespoons brown sugar
1 teaspoon sesame oil
1 teaspoon ground ginger
¼ teaspoon red pepper flakes
2 tablespoons sake
2 tablespoons vegetable oil
2 cloves garlic, chopped
1 onion, chopped
1 cup broccoli florets
1 cup carrots, peeled and sliced
½ cup red bell pepper, seeded and chopped
½ cup snow peas

Directions:
1. Cook the spaghetti in a large pot of boiling water for about 12 minutes. Drain and cool.
2. In a large Dutch oven, whisk the cornstarch into the vegetable stock until it dissolves. Add the peanut butter, soy sauce, honey, brown sugar, sesame oil, ginger and red pepper, whisking together. Bring this mixture to a boil, then simmer for five minutes until the sauce thickens. Stir in the sake and keep the mixture warm.
3. In a large skillet, heat the vegetable oil. Add the garlic and onion and sauté for three to five minutes, until the onion is tender.
4. Stir in the broccoli, carrots, bell pepper and snow peas, then reduce the heat.

5. Cover and steam, simmering about five minutes until everything is tender.
6. Toss together with the spaghetti and serve.

Anti-Inflammatory Diet

The anti-inflammatory diet is based on the theory that inflammation causes disease, so by reducing the inflammation in the body, wellness is achieved. When your body is dealing with any type of inflammation, it can lower your resistance to other maladies. Inflammation can increase inflammation, leaving you susceptible to serious conditions like heart disease, diabetes and cancer. Reducing inflammation by eating the right foods can have far-reaching effects.

The anti-inflammatory diet is based on a daily intake of 2000 to 3000 calories, about 50% of which comes from carbs, 30 percent from fat and 20 percent from protein.

Boost Your Immune System With Anti-Inflammatory Foods

This diet does allow meat, but in limited quantities. It focuses on fruits and dark leafy greens. It is based on the Mediterranean Diet, mentioned earlier in this chapter.

The anti-inflammatory diet is easy to follow and you can generally find something acceptable on just about any menu except for fast foods joints. You can easily locate a plethora of recipes, both in books and on the Internet. Most of the recipes in this book will apply to this diet as well.

Bok Choy Stir Fry

This recipe is meatless but the combination of mushrooms, peppers and a pile of bok choy make for a satisfying meal. Yield: three servings

Ingredients:

2 cups shitake mushrooms, chopped with stems removed
2 red peppers seeded and cut into thin strips
6 cups bok choy, chopped into 2 inch pieces
1 tablespoon coconut oil
1 yellow onion, chopped
4 cloves garlic, minced
1 tablespoon freshly-grated ginger root
2 teaspoons tamari sauce
1 teaspoon sesame oil
1 tablespoon fresh-squeezed lemon juice
¼ cup slivered or sliced almonds

Directions:

1. Cut the mushrooms, peppers and bok choy before beginning to cook.
2. Use a Dutch oven over medium-high heat to melt the coconut oil.
3. Add the onion and stir-fry for two to three minutes or until it softens.
4. Add the garlic and sauté for another minute.
5. Stir in the mushrooms and ginger, then cook for two more minutes.

6. Toss in the peppers and stir-fry for two minutes or until slightly softened.
7. In a bowl, whisk the tamari, sesame oil and lemon juice together. Pour it over the mixture in the pot and stir to combine all the ingredients.
8. Add the bok choy, cover the pot and let it steam for three to four minutes. Then serve while warm.

Red Lentil Squash Curry

This stew is full of protein and hearty flavors. It is designed to warm you up. You'll find this curry especially cheering in cold, blustery weather. Yield: four servings.

Ingredients:
1 teaspoon extra virgin olive oil
2 cloves garlic, minced
1 yellow onion, chopped
1 tablespoon curry powder (add more if you can take it)
1 cup red lentils
4 cups low-sodium vegetable broth
3 cups butternut squash, cooked and diced
1 cup collard greens
½ teaspoon salt
¼ teaspoon black pepper
1 tablespoon freshly grated ginger root

Directions:
1. Put a Dutch oven on the stove and heat the olive oil.
2. Add the garlic and onion and cook over medium-low heat until the onion is translucent.
3. Stir in the curry and cook for two minutes.
4. Add the broth and lentils and bring to a boil. As soon as it reaches a rolling boil, reduce the heat to a simmer and cook for 10 minutes, uncovered.
5. Stir in the cooked squash and greens.
6. Cover the pot and simmer over medium heat for about five minutes.

7. Season with salt and pepper, then add the ginger and serve it up hot.

Nutarian Diet

In this plant-based diet, you do not count calories. It includes superfoods and a reduced use of oils. This diet will produce weight loss and help you live a healthier life.

The Nutarian Diet Rates Foods From Good To Not Good

The diet promotes cruciferous greens along with other vegetables and fruits. It divides foods into four categories. Fruits and vegetables are on the top (most desirable) category and things you shouldn't consume (like soda) are on the bottom. The diet starts with a detox period that can be uncomfortable at first, but once you've overcome that hurdle you'll find you have enough food to keep you from getting hungry between meals. Membership is suggested and three membership tiers are available, tailored to almost anyone's budget. The diet is very specific regarding the dos and don'ts, which could be a bit of a challenge, but the benefits can be worth the hassle of learning the rules.

Peanut Slaw

The name for this slaw comes from the dressing, which includes natural peanut butter. The cabbage and carrots make it crunchy, even if you include no peanuts. This recipe is delicious and works well as a side dish. It makes four servings

Ingredients:

3 cups green cabbage, thinly sliced (use a combination of green and red cabbage if you wish)
2 large carrots, peeled and grated
1 green onion, thinly sliced
½ teaspoon low sodium soy sauce (See recipe, Chapter 11.) or liquid aminos (from a health food store)
2 teaspoons rice vinegar
3 tablespoons warm water
1 teaspoon lime juice
1 pinch cayenne pepper
2 tablespoons natural peanut butter

Directions:

1. Place the cabbage, carrots and green onion in a large serving bowl.
2. In a small bowl, whisk together the soy sauce, rice vinegar, water, lime juice and cayenne pepper.
3. Add the peanut butter and whisk vigorously until smooth. The warm water should help it smooth out.
4. Pour this mixture over the vegetables, toss to coat and serve.

Far From Old-Fashioned Green Bean Casserole

I love that old green bean casserole most people serve at Thanksgiving, but it is chock full of fat and sugar. This recipe provides a healthier substitute; you'll get less fat but fuller taste. It serves six.

Ingredients:

2 pounds fresh green beans, ends trimmed

2 tablespoons water
1 medium onion, thinly sliced
8 ounces mushrooms, washed and sliced
1 teaspoon garlic, minced
1 teaspoon low sodium soy sauce (See recipe, Chapter 11) or coconut aminos
⅛ teaspoon black pepper
⅛ teaspoon cayenne pepper
½ cup raw almonds
1 cup unsweetened almond milk (you can use soy or hemp milk), or slightly more to ensure the right consistency
¼ cup whole grain bread crumbs

Directions:

1. Blanch the green beans by placing them in boiling water and letting them boil for five minutes. Drain and place in the bottom of an oiled 9 by 9 inch casserole dish.
2. Place two tablespoons of water in a skillet over medium high heat; as soon as the skillet is hot, add the onions, mushrooms and garlic; sauté until the mushrooms have lost most of their liquid. Pour this on top of the green beans.
3. Place the soy sauce, black pepper, cayenne pepper, raw almonds and milk in a food processor or blender and blend on high until smooth. Pour over the green beans.
4. Sprinkle the breadcrumbs on top of the dish and set it in a preheated 350 degree Fahrenheit oven for 15 to 20 minutes or until bubbly and brown.

The Engine 2 Diet

This diet was created by Rip Esselstyn, a former firefighter and a triathlete. It was created out of concern for fellow firefighters with high cholesterol. This diet is plant based, shunning not only all animal products but vegetable oils as well. Mr. Esselstyn reports that the use of oils of any type in food preparation destroys many of the key nutrients in foods.

There are two diet introduction methods. The first involves a gradual adjustment, but the other is full force, hardcore and cold-turkey (with turkey excluded, of course). Engine 2 offers an extensive set of training videos and books. There is also a membership that doesn't cost a fortune but gives you unlimited access to heaps of information and offers a support community, which is almost essential, because this diet is very strict.

The Engine 2 Diet Helps You Move Into A Vegan Diet

Sweet Potato Bowl

This meal is tasty and colorful. It beckons you with orange, green, yellow and black components, daring you to dig in. Even if you adopt another form of diet, you will come back to this dish again and again. Note: you'll want to cook your sweet potato a day or so beforehand, so it is readily available for use. This recipe fills two bowls.

Ingredients:

1 large baked sweet potato, skin removed and cut into bite-sized cubes
1 can low sodium black beans, rinsed and drained
1 red bell pepper seeded and chopped
2 mangoes, peeled, seeded and chopped
1 avocado, peeled and chopped
1 cup cilantro, chopped
The juice of 1 lime
Balsamic vinegar to taste

Directions:
1. Warm the diced sweet potato and place it in a large bowl.
2. Add the black beans, bell pepper, mango and avocado and stir to combine.
3. Add the cilantro, lime juice and balsamic vinegar to taste and serve in two bowls.

Grilled Hummus Veggie Pizza

You will need a grill or grill pan for this recipe. It is so good, you will want more than just one. This recipe officially serves 4, but in my house it only serves 2. In other words, you may wish to double it...at least.

Ingredients:
1 tablespoon balsamic vinegar
1½ cups roasted red pepper hummus, divided (See recipe, Chapter 11.)
½ cup vegetable broth
2 Portobello mushroom caps, gills removed and cut into 1-inch strips
1 zucchini, sliced lengthwise into ⅓-inch planks
1 yellow squash, sliced lengthwise into ⅓-inch planks
4 tortillas (whole grain or brown rice)
¾ cup chopped fresh basil
8 ounces baby spinach, lightly steamed and squeezed to remove excess liquid
¼ cup pine nuts
1 pinch ground black pepper

Directions:
1. Whisk together the vinegar, a half cup of the hummus and all the broth in a large bowl. Add the mushrooms and toss to coat. Remove the mushrooms from the bowl with a slotted spoon and place in another container.
2. Put the zucchini and yellow squash in the bowl and toss to coat.
3. Return the mushrooms (you don't want to bruise them) and cover, letting them marinate at room temperature for 15 minutes up to an hour, but no longer.
4. Warm a grill or grill pan over medium heat. Grill the vegetables until browned and tender, three to four minutes on each side. Set the vegetables aside.
5. Place the tortillas on two baking pans covered with parchment paper. Spread each with a quarter cup of the remaining hummus. Top with basil and spinach and divide the grilled vegetables among the four tortillas.
6. Sprinkle with pine nuts and black pepper and set in the oven for 15 minutes or until the edges are brown and crisp. Then slice in half or fourths and serve while hot.

A Quick Overview

In summary, the Engine 2 and Nutarian diets are the most complicated to follow, although what you consider complex depends on where you're starting from. With any of these diets, if you are used to eating the things that are banned, you'll have more of a challenge from the start. I strongly recommend the Mediterranean diet because it is the most easily adopted of the plant-based diets. If you absolutely *must* add sweeteners to your food, consider the Flexitarian diet. For a well-balanced mix of carbohydrates, fats and protein, you might prefer the Anti-inflammatory diet. For a side-by-side comparison, you may value the following table.

Diet	Summary	Meat?	Dairy?	Fish?	How Complex?
Mediterranean	Fresh	Little	Yes	Little	Low
Flexitarian	Moderation in all (even sweetening)	Some	Some	Some	Low
Ornish	Good/bad foods and exercise	No	Maybe	yes	Medium
Vegetarian	Get Protein	Maybe (eggs)	Maybe	Maybe	Medium
Asian	Noodles, rice, veggies, fruit, nuts	Little	Rarely	Little	Low
Anti-Inflammatory	Balance	Limited	Cheese	Some	Medium
Nutarian	Good/Bad foods	None to little	None to little	<10%	High
Engine 2	No oils	No	No	No	High

Comparison Of Basic Plant-Based Diets

Choose your diet wisely, considering your food preferences, your activity level and how often you will be eating out during the day. Make a sample shopping list to ensure your chosen diet is affordable and lies within the amount of effort you want to put into it. Our next chapter will take you to the world of delicious and satisfying smoothies.

Chapter 3: Delicious and Healthy Smoothies

Who ever invented smoothies should get an award. These delicious beverages taste a bit like milkshakes, rich and sweet, but they don't load you down with sugar. Smoothies are a wonderful solution for days when you need to eat breakfast on the run. They're just as good for a quick lunch, although you never want to eat two smoothie meals in the same day.

Fruits and vegetables are a smoothie's mainstay, but just as important is the liquid used to make it. I do not use cow's milk, but I like the flavor of unsweetened coconut, almond, cashew or soy milk. You can use ground seeds, like flax and hemp to add it more nutrients and use chia seeds or protein powder to give you a bigger punch of protein.

I keep fruit ready to use by peeling it if needed, cutting it up, placing it in a freezer bag and storing it in the freezer for ready availability. Frozen fruits are what keep the smoothie thick and rich. I freeze halves of peeled bananas; they keep a lot longer than the fresh fruit. I also grind chia, flax and hemp seed in a coffee grinder so the nutrients will be better absorbed by your body, plus they will more easily blend into the smoothie.

You can flavor your smoothie with cocoa powder, cinnamon, nutmeg or any other spices. So, start your day with a delicious smoothie or take one to work and put it in the freezer until just before lunch. All these recipes produce one large smoothie or two small ones unless otherwise indicated.

Healthy Green Smoothie

This simple smoothie is full of vitamins and no extra stuff. Just vegetables and ice make for a delicious and detoxifying smoothie.

Ingredients:
2 cups baby spinach leaves, packed
1 stalk celery, cut in chunks
1 cucumber, peeled and cut in chunks
1/2 to 1 cup water or ice

Directions:
1. Place the spinach, celery and cucumber in a high speed blender and blend until smooth.
2. Add the water or ice and blend.

Chocolate Mint Smoothie

This smoothie is delicious and refreshing and tastes much like that certain cookie that comes for sale one time a year. It is a delicious-looking green color too. Make it just a mint smoothie by omitting the chocolate chips.

Ingredients:
¾ cup plain Greek Yogurt
1 cup almond milk
¼ cup fresh mint, tightly packed
1 cup baby spinach leaves
1 tablespoon maple syrup
¼ cup semi-sweet chocolate chips
2 cups ice

Directions:
1. Place the yogurt, milk, mint and spinach in a blender and blend on high until frothy.
2. Add the maple syrup and chocolate chips and blend a few seconds to break up the chocolate chips.

3. Add the ice and blend until thick and smooth.

Green Pumpkin Spice Smoothie

Pumpkin spice is all the rage in coffee, tea and other drinks during autumn, so why not in a smoothie. This smoothie tastes amazing and is a pretty green color too. Freeze your spinach overnight before making this smoothie for breakfast. Measure it out, put it in a freezer bag and go to bed.

Ingredients:
1 cup frozen spinach
1 cup unsweetened almond or coconut milk (more if too thick)
2 scoops vanilla protein powder
1 tablespoon smooth nut butter
1 teaspoon chia seed
1 teaspoon pumpkin pie spice

Directions:
1. Place the spinach in the blender and add the milk and protein powder. Blend to break up the spinach.

2. Add the nut butter, chia seed and spice and blend until smooth and thick. Add a little more milk if it is too thick.

Apple Spinach Protein Smoothie

Use A Tart Apple And Sprinkle Chia Seeds On Top

Spinach and apples might sound odd to some (I love spinach salad with tart apples in it), but it is very good as a smoothie. It tastes more like apple and spices than it does spinach. Fresh spinach does not have much flavor in a smoothie, so you can use as much as you want.

Ingredients:
½ cup rolled oats (not instant)
½ cup cold water
½ teaspoon cinnamon
½ teaspoon nutmeg
1 tablespoon almond butter
1 cup unsweetened almond milk, divided
1 scoop vanilla protein powder
1 large apple, cored, peeled and sliced
3 to 4 cups spinach leaves
4 to 5 ice cubes

Directions:

1. Place the oats and cold water in a blender and pulse a few times. Let it set for three to four minutes before proceeding.
2. Add the cinnamon, nutmeg and almond butter; pulse a few times to mix.
3. Pour in half a cup of almond milk and the protein powder and pulse.
4. Add the apple and blend until somewhat smooth.
5. Add the spinach leaves in two to three batches, blending until smooth each time.
6. Add the rest of the almond milk and the ice; then blend until thick.

Banana Berry Tropical Breeze

Feel the tropical breeze with these tropical flavors. You won't need ice if you freeze everything but the banana in this smoothie. It gives you a lovely tropical blend, thanks to the pineapple and banana.

Ingredients:

1 banana
¼ cup frozen pineapple
⅓ cup frozen raspberries
1 cup frozen strawberries
½ cup unsweetened almond milk.

Directions:

1. Place the banana in the blender along with the pineapple, raspberries and strawberries. Blend until almost smooth.
2. Add the almond milk and blend until smooth and creamy.

Banana Peanut Butter Cranberry Protein Smoothie

If you are looking for flavor, this is the smoothie for you. Banana and peanut butter are delicious together, but then add cranberry and you have a real treat. This smoothie is rich and full of antioxidants and vitamins. Cut and freeze your banana the night before; it will help the smoothie thicken up nicely.

Ingredients:
1 tablespoon chia seed, ground
1½ tablespoons hemp seed, ground
1 cup unsweetened coconut milk
2 tablespoons natural peanut butter or almond butter (See recipes, Chapter 11.)
1 banana, peeled, sliced and frozen
¼ cup dried cranberries
3 or 4 ice cubes
Shredded coconut (optional)

Directions:
1. Grind the chia and hemp seed in a coffee grinder and add them to the coconut milk in the blender. Pulse to combine the seeds and milk.
2. Add the peanut butter, frozen banana slices and dried cranberries and blend to combine until smooth.
3. Add the ice cubes one by one and blend in to thicken the smoothie. You may only have to use three of the four. Sprinkle with some shredded coconut if desired.

Blueberry Oatmeal Protein Smoothie

Blueberries are a Superfood And Delicious

This bright blue smoothie will keep you full and energetic all the way to lunch. Soaking the oatmeal in a liquid for three to four minutes allows it to soften, so do not skip this step, or you'll have a chunky, not-so-appetizing smoothie.

Ingredients:
½ cup water
½ cup rolled oats (not instant)
1 cup unsweetened coconut or almond milk
1 cup blueberries, frozen
4 ice cubes
1 scoop vanilla protein powder
2 tablespoons chia seed, ground in a coffee grinder
1 tablespoon almond butter (See recipe, Chapter 11.)

Directions:
1. Combine the water, oatmeal and coconut or almond milk in the blender and pulse a few times. Let sit for three to four minutes.

2. Add the blueberries and ice cubes and blend until just combined.
3. Add the protein powder, ground chia seeds and almond butter. Blend until everything is smooth and thick. Add more ice if needed to balance the consistency.

Carrot Orange Ginger Smoothie

This smoothie is bright orange in color and full of rich nutrients. Carrots and oranges really do taste good together, especially when combined with the spiciness of ginger. I unusually peel my orange and separate the sections then freeze them. This gives the smoothie enough coldness to thicken up a little.

Ingredients:
2 tablespoons flax seeds, ground
½ cup unsweetened coconut milk
2 oranges, peeled, sections separated and frozen
1 inch ginger, peeled and grated
2 large carrots, peeled then cut into small chunks

Directions:
1. Grind the chia seeds with a coffee grinder and place them in the blender.
2. Pour in the coconut milk and frozen orange segments; pulse to mix until chunky.
3. Add the ginger and carrots, blending until smooth and creamy.

Chocolate-Strawberry Heaven

Enjoy Rich Chocolate And Sumptuous Strawberries

When my mom used to make homemade chocolate pudding, she would garnish it with fresh, sliced strawberries. That's when I learned that chocolate and strawberries go quite well together.

This smoothie reminds me of home and mom's best comfort food. You'll also find it can calm your chocolate cravings. So, dig in!

Ingredients:
 1 tablespoon chia seeds, ground
 1 cup almond milk
 1 scoop chocolate protein powder
 2 tablespoons raw almonds
 1 cup frozen, sliced strawberries

Directions:

1. Grind the chia seeds and place them in a blender with the almond milk.
2. Add the chocolate protein powder and almonds and pulse mix everything together.
3. Add the strawberries and blend until smooth and rich and thick.

Cherry Limeade Smoothie

I use pitted sour cherries or Bing cherries, both from right off the tree, to make this smoothie. It yields a little more than usual, with two medium servings. The peach neutralizes the flavors and adds a bit of sweetness to the smoothie. The recipe calls for frozen cherries; I usually measure mine and freeze it the night before, but you can also use a cup of fresh cherries and add a little ice.

Ingredients:

1 heaping cup of frozen pitted cherries
1 ripe peach, peeled and sliced
1 tablespoon ground chia seeds
1 cup almond milk
1 to 2 limes, juiced
1 handful of ice

Directions:

1. Add the cherries and peach slices to the blender and pulse.
2. Add the ground chia seeds and pulse.
3. Pour in the almond milk, lime juice and ice; blend until smooth and thick. Add ice if more thickness is needed.

Layered Smoothie

Delicious Combination Of Kiwi-Spinach And Orange-Mango

This smoothie is a partial rainbow in a glass. It comes out with three layers: orange-yellow, pink and green. I use either two teaspoons of powdered stevia or one tablespoon of agave syrup to sweeten this treat. You could also use a peeled, chopped banana for sweetness. You'll make each flavor separately so divide the milk and sweetener into three equal amounts.

Ingredients:

1¼ cups frozen mango pieces
1 cup almond milk, divided
2 teaspoons stevia, 1 tablespoon agave syrup or, 1 peeled banana, divided into 3 parts
1 cup frozen strawberries, hulled and cut in half
1 cup fresh spinach

Directions:

1. Place the mango pieces in the blender, pour in a third of the milk and add a third of the sweetener. Blend until smooth, then pour into the bottom of a large glass.
2. Place the strawberries in the blender along with another third of the milk and the sweetener; blend this until smooth. Pour gently over the mango layer in the glass.
3. Place the spinach and the remaining milk and sweetener in the blender and blend until smooth. Pour on top of the strawberry layer.

Eat Your Kale Smoothie

Kale is not my favorite vegetable, but it does contain a great deal of precious nutrients. Instead of eating your kale, why not drink it in a smoothie? This one tastes more like banana and berries than kale. This way you can get the benefits of kale without gagging on the taste.

This smoothie calls for water instead of milk and makes two small to medium servings.

Ingredients:
½ cup frozen mixed berries, (I use raspberries, strawberries, blueberries and blackberries)
1 medium ripe banana, peeled and frozen
2 cups fresh kale, stems removed
1 heaping tablespoon hemp seed, ground
⅔ cup pomegranate juice
¾ to 1½ cups water

Directions:
1. Place the frozen berries and banana in a blender and pulse to break up.
2. Add the kale and blend until somewhat smooth
3. Add the hemp seed, pomegranate juice and a quarter cup of water, blending until smooth. If your smoothie is too thick at this point, add water a bit at a time until you get the consistency you like.

Green Apple Orange Banana Spice

As you can see, this smoothie has a variety of ingredients. Of course kale, with its massive protein content, is included; yet this recipe does a good job of hiding the flavor. (My half-hearted apologies go out to those of you who love "essence of kale.")

Ingredients:
1 medium Granny Smith apple, cut into slices
1 cup orange juice
1 banana, peeled, sliced and frozen
1½ cup kale
1 teaspoon ginger root, peeled and minced
1 tablespoon chia or flax seed, ground
½ teaspoon ground cinnamon

Directions:
1. Place the apple in the blender and pulse to break it up.
2. Add the orange juice and frozen banana slices and pulse again to break up and roughly combine.
3. Add the kale and blend.
4. Add the gingerroot, chia or flax seed and cinnamon; blend until smooth and thick.

Maple Fig Smoothie

Figs Have An Intriguing Color And Texture, Inside And Out

Figs have a sweet and musky flavor that I love. When you combine them with chocolate, you get a decadently rich smoothie. This recipe makes about three cups in quantity. It is quite rich however, so you won't really *need* as much as with other smoothies. If you limit your sugar intake you might want to steer clear of this smoothie, as it includes maple syrup along with the natural fruit sugars.

Ingredients:
¾ cup rolled oats
1 cup preferred milk
6 to 8 figs, stemmed and cut in half
1 banana, peeled, cut into slices and frozen
2 tablespoons almond, cashew, or peanut butter
1 pinch ground ginger
1 pinch cinnamon
1 pinch cayenne pepper
¼ cup cocoa powder
¼ cup coconut oil
¼ cup maple syrup

Directions:

1. Combine the oats and milk in the blender, pulse and let set for about two minutes.
2. Add the figs and banana slices and pulse.
3. Add the nut butter, ginger, cinnamon and cayenne pepper; blend until smooth.
4. In a bowl, combine the cocoa powder, coconut oil and maple syrup. Whisk until thoroughly mixed, then pour most of it into the blender and blend until smooth and creamy.
5. Divide among individual glasses, drizzling the rest of the syrup on top as an artistic garnish.

Mint Protein Smoothie

Mint Is Super-Refreshing

Mint is a cooling flavor on a hot day. It is also good all year round, to kick up the flavor of most dishes.

I grow mint in a large pot (to prevent it from taking over my garden). This means I always have plenty of fresh mint available in the summer. I love to mix it with fruit and tropical blends.

For this smoothie I always use coconut milk because it matches up with a tropical theme. This smoothie is filled with nutrients from the fruit and full of protein because of the chia, hemp and flax seeds, so get your coffee grinder out and start grinding.

Ingredients:
    1 tablespoon chia seeds, ground
    1 tablespoon hemp seeds, ground
    1 tablespoon flax seed, ground
    ½ cup mango pieces, frozen
    1 large orange, peeled and sectioned
    1 banana, peeled, chopped in pieces and frozen
    1 scoop vanilla protein powder
    ¾ cup unsweetened coconut milk
    5 to 6 fresh mint leaves

Directions:
    1. Grind the chia, hemp and flax seed and place them in a blender.
    2. Add the frozen mango, the orange sections and the frozen banana pieces to the blender and pulse a few times.
    3. Add the protein powder and coconut milk; pulse again to combine.
    4. Add the mint leaves and blend until smooth. If the smoothie is too runny, add a few ice cubes and blend again until thick and smooth.

Orange Blueberry Madness

Orange and blueberries don't really seem to go together, but they do. That's the reason for the "Madness" in the title. When I first tasted this smoothie, I thought, "What madness is this?" It tasted wonderful! It also kept me from getting hungry until lunch time, so it truly contains a touch of madness.

You can use fresh or frozen blueberries, but you're going to freeze them overnight, anyhow. I measure mine out in cup-sized portions before freezing; that means they're ready to go when I'm ready to make them.

Ingredients:

1 cup blueberries, frozen
1 orange, peeled and sectioned
1 cup almond or coconut milk
1 scoop vanilla protein powder
1 teaspoon ground nutmeg
1 tablespoon shredded coconut

Directions:
1. Place the orange sections and blueberries in the blender and pulse a few times to break them up.
2. Add the milk, protein powder and nutmeg; blend until smooth and creamy.
3. Sprinkle the coconut on top if you like, but honestly, it's just as tasty without.

Peachy Keen Smoothie

No One Can Resist A Peach Smoothie

This smoothie is my go-to treat when I get a craving for my favorite dessert – peach pie. It's full of peachy flavor with a hint of citrus. If you desire more sweetness, you can add a tablespoon of powdered stevia or agave syrup.

This recipe makes two smoothies.

Ingredients:

½ cup unsweetened almond milk (optional substitution: coconut milk)

¼ cup rolled oats

1 teaspoon ground chia seeds

2 ripe peaches, pitted, skinned and cut into slices

¼ cup fresh orange juice

½ frozen banana, peeled and cut into sections before freezing

Directions:

1. Place the almond milk, rolled oats and chia seeds in the blender and pulse a few times. Let it set for two to three minutes.
2. Add the peaches, orange juice and the frozen banana pieces and blend until smooth and creamy.
3. If you want to add sweetener, add it and blend in.

Pear Basil Citrus Smoothie

Pears have a mild flavor, which means you you'll need other ways to punch up the flavor on this smoothie. Stronger flavors like basil and citrus work well, because the pear tones them down and still comes shining through.

This smoothie contains no milk or other liquid, only the lemon juice and celery juice. This gives it a uniquely refreshing flavor that is packed with vitamins and other nutrients that are largely anti-inflammatory.

Ingredients:

4 large stalks celery, juiced (only use the juice; discard the solids)

8 ounces sliced pear

¼ cup fresh squeezed lemon juice

1 cup fresh basil leaves

Directions:

1. Juice the celery stalks and pour the juice into the blender.
2. Add the lemon juice and pear slices and blend until smooth.
3. Add the basil leaves and blend again until smooth. If the smoothie appears runny, blend in ice a little at a time until it reaches your preferred consistency.

Purple People Eater Smoothie

This Purple Smoothie Catches Everyone's Attention

A song about a "one-eyed, one-horned flying purple people eater" made the charts back in the 1950s. The record cover (yes, vinyl!) displayed a dragon that was about the color of this smoothie.

You don't have to worry about a purple people eater coming to your home to be able to enjoy this sweet potato based smoothie. The recipe makes two. It might turn your tongue a little purple, but that's all, other than giving you a great nutritional boost.

Ingredients:

2 lavender tea bags or 2 teaspoons of loose lavender tea in a diffuser

¼ cup boiled water

1 cup purple sweet potato, cooked and peeled (about 1 large potato)

1 cup blueberries, frozen

1½ tablespoons maple syrup

3 to 4 tablespoons almond or coconut milk

2 tablespoons vanilla yogurt

Directions:

1. Boil a quarter cup of water and pour into a mug, adding the tea. Cover and let it steep for 10 minutes. Remove the bags or the diffuser. Let the tea cool to room temperature.
2. Meanwhile, boil the whole sweet potato in water for about 20 minutes. Let it cool enough to handle and peel. Cut the potato up and measure out one cup. Let the potato cool to room temperature.
3. Place the cooled potato in the blender and add the blueberries. Pulse the mixture to break everything up.
4. Add the maple syrup and milk, one tablespoon at a time, until you reach the right consistency. You may only need two tablespoons or you might need all four.
5. Swirl in the yogurt by spooning it into the blender and pulsing quickly. Pour into glasses and enjoy.

Raspberry Green Grape Smoothie

This smoothie packs a punch with Vitamins C and K. The zucchini does not add flavor but it does thicken the smoothie. The flavor of raspberries combined with green grapes is exceptional.

You can add an avocado to help thicken the smoothie, but while some people like the flavor it adds to the flavor and I don't particularly care for it.

This smoothie is made a little differently. You make it the night before and pour it into ice cube trays. In the morning you pop out the frozen cubes and blend it up. You can actually do this with any smoothie if you want. Just freeze it in cubes and you'll have a frostie ready to eat in minutes with no measuring and pre-blending.

This recipe makes up about two cups of smoothie, so drink a big one or share with a friend.

Ingredients:
2 tablespoons chia seeds, ground
2 cups raspberries
1 cup green grapes
1 peeled zucchini, cut into chunks
½ cup almond milk
¼ cup or less, water (see instructions)
½ avocado (optional)

Directions:
1. Grind the chia seeds and place them in the blender.
2. Add the raspberries and green grapes and pulse to break up.
3. Add the zucchini and almond milk and blend until smooth.
4. Add the water, a tablespoon or two at a time, blending until the right consistency is reached.
5. If the smoothie does not thicken up, add the avocado and blend until it is smooth.
6. Pour the mixture into ice cube trays. In the morning pop out as many as you like and blend until smooth.

Raspberry Quinoa Coconut Smoothie

Raspberries, quinoa, goji berries and coconut are all considered superfoods that can help keep your body healthy. The Medjool date is what gives the smoothie its flavor and some of its nutritional value.

Ingredients:

1 cup coconut milk
½ cup cooked quinoa
1 Medjool date
1 cup raspberries
2 tablespoons dried goji berries
2 tablespoons shredded coconut

Directions:

1. Pour the coconut milk into the blender and add the cooked quinoa. Let the mixture sit for a minute or two before pulsing to blend.
2. Pit the date and cut it into chunks. Add it to the blender with the raspberries, goji berries and coconut.
3. Blend on high until smooth and creamy.

Spicy Oatmeal Banana Smoothie

This smoothie is thick and rich. It is made with turmeric, a spice with a unique flavor but full of valuable nutrients. The cinnamon and ginger will add a little kick of flavor.

Ingredients:

1 banana, peeled, cut into sections and frozen
1 cup almond milk
¼ cup rolled oats
½ teaspoon ground cinnamon
¼ teaspoon ground ginger
¼ teaspoon ground turmeric

Directions:

1. Freeze the banana overnight and put it in the blender in the morning.
2. Pour the almond milk into the blender and add in the banana and the rolled oats. Pulse to combine slightly; let the mixture set for two or three minutes, allowing the milk to soak into the oats.
3. Add the cinnamon, ginger and turmeric; blend until smooth and creamy.

Tropical Citrus Peach Smoothie

Add Grated Ginger To This Tropical Smoothie For Greater Punch

Mixing peaches with tropical fruits will make your taste buds happy. This smoothie is easy to make the night before for a breakfast treat.

Ingredients:

1 orange, peeled and sectioned
¼ cup pineapple pieces
1 large banana, peeled, sliced in sections and frozen
1 cup frozen mango pieces
½ cup frozen peach slices
¼ cup almond or coconut milk
Ice cubes

Directions:

1. Peel the orange and separate the segments. Place them in a blender.
2. Add the pineapple pieces and pulse.
3. Add the frozen mango and peach pieces and pulse.
4. Pour in the almond milk and blend on high, adding ice as needed thicken the consistency.

Turmeric Overnight Oatmeal Smoothie

Turmeric is now being hailed as a form of heal-all. It has the ability to prevent and banish infections, heal wounds, balance blood sugar, remove joint stiffness and minimize aches and pains. At the same time it functions as a spice, most often found in Indian and Asian cuisines.

Turmeric stains anything it touches, turning foods a bright yellow. I use it generously in much of my cooking, as a thyroid stimulant. If this cheery-colored smoothie doesn't lift your spirits, I don't know what will.

Ingredients:
   1 cup rolled oats
   ½ cup water
   1 teaspoon lemon juice
   2 cups mango pieces, frozen
   1 teaspoon ground chia seed
   1 cup coconut milk
   1 teaspoon ground turmeric
   3 tablespoons shredded coconut

Directions:
   1. In a cup or bowl, combine the oats with the water and lemon juice. Cover and put in the refrigerator overnight.
   2. Place the rolled oat mixture in a blender; add the mango and the ground chia seeds. Pulse a few times.
   3. Add the coconut milk, turmeric and shredded coconut. Blend on high until smooth and creamy.

Smoothies are great for breakfast, but if you want something plant-based that is a little more substantial to sink your teeth into, go on to the next chapter. There you'll find all sorts of delicious plant-based breakfast dishes.

Chapter 4: Breakfast Meals To Start Your Day Off Right

How many times have you eaten a doughnut for breakfast and about 10:30 a.m. your tummy starts to rumble? Those doughnuts are full of sugar, addictive sugar that just makes you want even more. Eat one and immediately your blood sugar spikes through the roof and you're full of pizazz; you're revved up and ready to handle anything life can throw at you. But that's not all. Just when you've settled into your new plane of existence the mirage begins to fade. You've used up all that energy; now your sugar levels come crashing down, leaving you tired, even hungrier and grumpy because you're craving your next sugar fix.

I'm sorry to start the chapter off with such a sad story. However, it's best to warn you up front to stay away from sugary foods in the morning and instead opt for a plant-based breakfast. It'll keep you from gnawing on the furniture mid-morning and you'll sustain your scintillating personality all the way to lunchtime.

They say that breakfast is the most important meal of the day, but if you are like me, your stomach just might not be ready for solid food early in the morning. I prefer to eat breakfast around nine or so. If I *must* be functional earlier, I'll often take my breakfast along with me.

Now for the *good* news; many of the breakfast entrees in this chapter can be eaten on the go or carried with you to eat later. (Lunch, anyone?) Some you can even put together the night beforehand.

Apple Pumpkin Seed Muffins

Apple Pumpkin Seed Muffins Will Start Your Day Off Right

This recipe calls for an apple puree that is easily made by peeling and coring three large apples and chopping them up. You'll simply toss the chunks into a blender and process the apples until they look like a bunch of lumpy baby food. You don't want to liquefy it nor smooth it out completely, because part of the delight of this muffin is biting into a small chunk of apple and getting a sweet burst of flavor.

This recipe makes six muffins. It's easiest to make in autumn when you can get raw pumpkin seeds straight out of the pumpkin. Otherwise, you'll want to use packaged pumpkin seeds that have been lightly salted or not salted at all.

Ingredients:
    2 cups whole-wheat flour
    1 teaspoon baking soda
    1 teaspoon baking powder
    ⅛ teaspoon sea salt
    1 teaspoon ground cinnamon
    ½ cup raw pumpkin seeds
    1 cup raisins

1½ cups apple puree (made yourself as above)
1 teaspoon lemon zest
1 tablespoon fresh lemon juice)
⅓ cup maple syrup
½ cup almond or soy milk (adjust the amount as needed)

Directions:
1. Preheat the oven to 350 degrees, Fahrenheit and prepare a muffin tin with nonstick spray or paper cupcake cups. You will use only six of the cups.
2. In a bowl, whisk together the flour, baking soda, baking powder, cinnamon and salt.
3. Add the pumpkin seed and raisins and stir in.
4. Pour in the apple puree and combine well.
5. Add the lemon zest, lemon juice and maple syrup; mix thoroughly.
6. Add the milk, a tablespoon at a time, until you reach the right consistency.
7. Pour the batter into six muffin cups, dividing the batter equally. Bake for 35 to 40 minutes or until a toothpick inserted in the center of one muffin comes out clean.
8. Let your muffins cool for 15 minutes before removing from the pan.
9. Eat warm or let the muffins cool to room temperature for future use.

Avocado Flatbread

If you like avocados, you will love this flatbread, which you make yourself. Some of the ingredients below are only found in health food stores, but they are plant-based and gluten free. This recipe makes four flatbreads.

Ingredients:
½ cup chickpea flour (See recipe, Chapter 11)
½ cup gluten free flour
¼ teaspoon xanthum gum
½ cup tapioca starch (a.k.a., tapioca flour), divided
¼ teaspoon salt

1 tablespoon canola oil
½ cup water, more if needed
2 tablespoons avocado oil
1 avocado, thinly sliced

Directions:
1. Whisk together in a large bowl the chickpea flour, gluten free flour, xanthum gum, a quarter cup of the tapioca starch and salt.
2. Add the canola oil and stir well.
3. Add the water a little at a time while stirring, until the dough reaches the right consistency. It should be sticky and form a ball.
4. Sprinkle the remaining tapioca starch on a clean flat surface and knead it into the dough. Add the starch and continue to knead until the dough is smooth and elastic. Divide into four balls.
5. Roll one ball on the starched surface, flattening it and rolling it out to between six and eight inches in diameter. The shape can be round or oblong.
6. Heat the avocado oil in a large skillet over medium high heat. Place the flatbread in the skillet and fry it on one side for about a minute, until the edges brown and bubble. Flip your flatbread and fry the other side. When lightly brown on the second side, remove it to a platter and repeat the process for the remaining balls of dough
7. Top with sliced avocado and serve while warm.

Banana Breakfast Bars With A Blueberry Twist

These are great for days you find yourself hitting the ground running. You can snack on one or two as you head out the door in the morning. They also make a great midmorning snack.

The bars are sweetened with dates and apple juice. You can use either fresh or frozen blueberries with this recipe. It will make about 12 bars.

Ingredients:

1½ cups apple juice
1 cup dates, pitted and cut into half
3 cups old-fashion rolled oats, divided
¼ teaspoon nutmeg
¼ teaspoon cinnamon
1 teaspoon vanilla extract (See recipe, Chapter 11.)
2 ripe bananas, peeled
1 cup blueberries
½ cup walnuts or pecans

Directions:

1. Pour the apple juice in a bowl and add the dates. Soak for 15 minutes.
2. Preheat the oven to 375 degrees, Fahrenheit and prepare a nine by nine inch baking pan with parchment paper that extends to the top of the pan on all sides. Cut slits in the corners to allow the paper to lay flat.
3. Pour two cups of rolled oats in a medium bowl and add the nutmeg and cinnamon. Whisk together until mixed, then set the bowl aside.
4. Place the vanilla and bananas in the blender. Use a slotted spoon to remove the dates from the apple juice to a small bowl. Pour the apple juice and remaining rolled oats into the blender and blend until smooth and creamy.
5. Add the soaked dates and pulse until chunky. You will want small chunks of date in your batter.
6. Add this mixture to the blender, on top of the rolled oat and spice mixture; mix well. Fold in the blueberries and the nuts, working gently to avoid squashing the berries.
7. Pour the batter into the prepared baking pan and bake for 30 to 35 minutes or until a toothpick comes out clean when inserted in the middle.
8. Cool for 10 to 15 minutes before cutting into bars. Serve warm or cold; store any remaining bars in an airtight container.

Banana Peach Bread

Quick Breads Make A Quick And Nutritious Breakfast Option

Quick bread is easy to make and it makes for a great quick breakfast in the morning. This recipe includes both peaches and bananas, giving off a lovely aroma and a delicious flavor to wake up to in the morning. It does contain some sugar, but I use the healthier raw sugar instead of the highly processed granulated form. The batter is mixed by hand, minimizing your cleanup afterwards. This recipe makes one loaf.

Ingredients:

1 banana, peeled
½ cup canola oil
¾ cup applesauce (See recipe, Chapter 11)
½ cup sugar
2 teaspoons vanilla extract (See recipe, Chapter 11.)
3 cups wheat flour
1 teaspoon baking soda
1 teaspoon baking powder
1 teaspoon salt
3 teaspoons cinnamon
2 cups diced peaches, fresh or canned and drained

Directions:

1. Preheat the oven to 350 degrees, Fahrenheit and grease a regular loaf pan.
2. Place the peeled banana in a large bowl and crush with a fork.
3. Add the canola oil, applesauce, sugar and vanilla, stirring to mix well.
4. In another bowl, whisk together the flour, baking soda, baking powder, salt and cinnamon. Gradually add and stir into the banana mixture by hand.
5. Stir in the peaches and pour the batter into the prepared loaf pan.
6. Bake for one and a half hours or until a toothpick inserted in the center of the loaf comes out clean.
7. Cool in the pan, remove and slice.

Black Beans with Orange Breakfast Tacos

Want something a little different, yet quite tasty, for breakfast? This will quickly become a favorite. You can easily create the filling the night before. The only thing you'll need to do in the morning is heat the filling, warm the tortillas, fill the tacos and eat them. This recipe makes about six tacos.

Ingredients:

1 teaspoon olive oil
½ cup onion, diced
½ cup mushrooms, chopped
½ cup fresh corn kernels (or frozen, thawed and drained)
¾ cup black beans (half of a can)
⅛ cup nutritional yeast (optional)
¼ teaspoon chili powder
¼ teaspoon paprika
¼ teaspoon sea salt
¼ teaspoon ground black pepper
2 tablespoons orange juice
1 package corn tortillas
½ cup lettuce or fresh spinach
1 tomato, diced

1 avocado, thinly sliced

Directions:

1. Heat the oil in a skillet over medium high heat and sauté the onion, mushrooms, corn and black beans for four to five minutes or until they soften slightly.
2. Add the yeast, if you're using it, along with the chili powder, paprika, salt, pepper and orange juice. Mash with a potato masher, but make sure to leave it slightly chunky. Stir and heat until the mixture is heated through. Cover the mixture and set it aside.
3. In a skillet coated with nonstick spray, heat the corn tortillas for a minute or two on each side, just long enough to warm and slightly brown them.
4. Fold the tortillas and add the filling. Top with fresh greens, tomatoes and avocado.

Chia Carrot Coconut Breakfast Pudding

Sliced Bananas Add An Extra Treat

I cannot adequately describe the flavor of this pudding. It is fresh, spicy and almost tropical, with a wafting of nutty flavor. All I know for sure is that it tastes scrumptious and I have a hard time stopping after one bowlful. I prepare mine the night before, so it has plenty of time to stew in its juices. All that's left to do in the morning is add a few ingredients. This recipe will give you two large bowl full or four smaller bowls. Go ahead; indulge yourself!

Ingredients:
1 teaspoon cinnamon
3 tablespoons chia seeds
4 tablespoons old-fashioned rolled oats
½ cup carrot juice
1 cup coconut milk
1 tablespoon peanut, almond, or cashew butter (See recipe, Chapter 11.)
1 banana, sliced
Maple Syrup (optional)

Directions:
1. In a bowl, combine the cinnamon, chia seeds, rolled oats, carrot juice and coconut milk. Cover and store in the refrigerator overnight.
2. Remove from the refrigerator and let sit on the counter for about 15 minutes.
3. Add the peanut butter and mix it in well.
4. Add the sliced banana on top and drizzle with maple syrup.

Cinnamon Orange Quinoa Breakfast Pudding

This pudding is served warm; it'll wake you up with strong flavors that pop in your mouth. The recipe does call for sugar, but I use raw sugar or a tablespoon of honey instead of granulated sugar. Agave syrup would work as well. This makes a big bowlful, which I love to share.

Ingredients:
1 cup quinoa

2 tablespoons fresh squeezed orange juice
2½ cups vanilla flavored almond milk
1 tablespoon sugar
¾ teaspoon cinnamon
¼ teaspoon nutmeg
1 tablespoon orange zest

Directions:

1. Place the uncooked quinoa, orange juice and milk in a saucepan over medium heat.
2. Stir in the sugar, cinnamon, nutmeg and orange zest.
3. Let the mixture come to a rolling bowl, then let it boil for one minute.
4. Turn the heat down to a simmer, cover the pot and let it alone for 20 minutes. I usually look in on the contents halfway through, just to give it a stir and check to see that it isn't burning on the bottom.
5. Serve hot with more orange zest and dried cranberries or raisins sprinkled on top.

Cranberry Raisin Oatmeal

Try Honey Instead Of Maple Syrup For A Different Flavor

I love dried cranberries and am never happier than when they can be found on the shelves of my grocery store. Here is a tasty way to use those cranberries and start your day out right. The recipe yields four servings, so everyone in the family can have their own bowlful of tasty plant-based goodness.

Ingredients:

2 cups old-fashioned oats
1½ tablespoons raisins
1½ tablespoons dried cranberries
⅛ teaspoon sea salt
1½ tablespoons maple syrup
Sunflower seeds

Almond milk

Directions:
1. In a saucepan, combine the oats, raisins, cranberries, water and salt. Stir and bring to a boil.
2. Reduce the heat to medium low and stir occasionally until most of the liquid has been absorbed.
3. Remove from the heat and add the maple syrup, stirring in well.
4. Pour into bowls and sprinkle with some sunflower seeds and a splash of milk.

Crustless Broccoli Tomato Quiche

This Quiche Has No Eggs, But Instead, Tofu

This quiche is scrumptious, even though it's made using tofu and roasted vegetables. It serves four and is made in a 9-inch pie pan or a springform pan.

Ingredients:
1½ cups fresh broccoli, chopped
2 leeks, cleaned and sliced, using all the white and a little green
2 tablespoons vegetable broth
1 12.8-ounce box extra firm tofu, drained and dried

2 cloves garlic, chopped
1 lemon, juiced
2 teaspoons yellow mustard
1 tablespoon tahini sauce
1 tablespoon cornstarch
¼ cup old-fashioned oats
3 to 4 dashes Tabasco sauce
½ teaspoon turmeric
½ teaspoon salt
⅔ cup sun-dried tomatoes soaked in hot water and drained, then chopped
½ cup artichoke hearts, chopped
⅛ cup additional vegetable broth

Directions:

1. Preheat the oven to 375 degrees, Fahrenheit and prepare a nine-inch pie pan by coating it with nonstick spray. Set aside.
2. Cover a baking sheet with parchment paper and coat with nonstick spray. Place the chopped broccoli and sliced leeks on the sheet and drizzle with the two tablespoons of vegetable broth. Season with a little salt and pepper and toss with the hands to coat. Bake for 20 to 30 minutes until the vegetables are roasted. Remove from the oven and set aside.
3. Place In a food processor the tofu, garlic, lemon juice, mustard, tahini, cornstarch, rolled oats, tobacco sauce, turmeric and salt. Process until smooth.
4. In a big bowl, combine the roasted vegetables, the drained sun dried tomatoes and the artichoke hearts. Add the tofu mixture to the vegetable mixture and mix well with a rubber spatula.
5. Add the broth and combine well.
6. Scrape into the pie pan and flatten out the mixture. Bake for 30 to 35 minutes or until light brown. Cool for 15 minutes before slicing.

Flax meal Zucchini Cakes

Zucchini Cakes Are Deliciously Colorful

These pancakes contain a bunch of nutritious ingredients, things like zucchini, chickpeas and flaxseed. I serve them with a little mango chutney on top, but you can also use maple syrup or honey. This recipe serves four people.

Ingredients:

3 tablespoons water
1 tablespoon ground flaxseed
⅓ of a 15-ounce can of chickpeas, mostly mashed but some whole
2 medium zucchini, grated
2 tablespoons red onion, grated
3 tablespoons wheat flour
¼ cup cornmeal
1 teaspoon baking powder
⅛ teaspoon salt

Directions:

1. Pour the water in a large bowl and add the flaxseed. Set aside and let soak for 10 minutes

2. Mash the chickpeas and add them to the flaxseed bowl along with the red onion and grated zucchini. Stir to combine well.
3. In another bowl whisk together the flour, cornmeal, baking powder and salt.
4. Gradually add the flour mixture to the chickpea mixture to make a batter.
5. Coat a skillet with nonstick spray and use three tablespoons each of the batter to form pancakes in the skillet. Cook each pancake for two minutes on each side and serve with chutney or syrup.

Fruit-topped Buckwheat Pancakes

Use Any Available Fruit To Top These Pancakes

Buckwheat flour, cornmeal and oatmeal are the base for these pancakes; they're sweetened with bananas and applesauce. Sprinkle with your choice of chopped nuts and maple syrup or top with fresh blueberries. This recipe will serve 3.

Ingredients:
1 cup buckwheat flour
½ cup old-fashioned rolled oats
½ cup cornmeal
1 teaspoon cinnamon
1 teaspoon baking powder
1 teaspoon baking soda
½ teaspoon salt

1 large banana
1 to 1½ cups almond milk or coconut milk
½ cup applesauce (See recipe, Chapter 11)
1 teaspoon vanilla (See recipe, Chapter 11.)

Directions:

1. Mix the buckwheat flour, oatmeal, cornmeal, cinnamon, baking powder, baking soda and salt in a large bowl and whisk to combine well. Set the bowl aside.
2. Peel and mash the banana in another large bowl. Add one cup milk, applesauce and vanilla and stir to combine. If it seems too thick, add more of the milk, up to a half cup.
3. Gradually add the buckwheat mixture to the banana mixture, beating with a spoon after each addition until the batter is well mixed. Let it set for five minutes.
4. Heat a skillet, coat it with nonstick butter flavored spray and drop two large spoonfuls in the pan to make one pancake. Once it browns on the edges and stops bubbling, flip it to the other side and cook until brown.
5. Remove to a platter and continue making pancakes with the remaining batter.
6. Serve, topped with maple syrup, more applesauce, chutney, or blueberries and bananas.

German Chocolate Pancakes

This recipe makes 12 of the most delicious pancakes ever. They taste much like a slice of German chocolate cake. The mashed banana and maple syrup are what makes the pancakes sweet. The topping emulates German chocolate frosting, made with sweet pecan butter, dates, coconut and pecans.

Ingredients:

¾ cup medjool dates
½ cup mashed banana
1¼ cups coconut milk
2 teaspoons vanilla extract (See recipe, Chapter 11.)
¼ teaspoon sea salt
1½ cups gluten free flour

¼ cup unsweetened cocoa powder

2 teaspoons baking powder

3 tablespoons maple syrup

3 tablespoons pecan or almond butter (See recipe, Chapter 11.)

1 teaspoon more vanilla extract

1 pinch sea salt

⅓ cup water (more or less)

⅓ cup chopped pecans

⅓ cup shredded coconut

Directions:

1. Soak the dates for 30 minutes in enough water to cover them.
2. Use a food processor to lightly combine the mashed banana, coconut milk and vanilla by pulsing.
3. In a bowl, mix a quarter teaspoon of sea salt with the flour, cocoa and baking powder; gradually add to the banana mixture in the processor, pulsing to combine and processing until smooth.
4. Add the maple syrup while the processor is running.
5. Grease a skillet with coconut oil and add the batter, a quarter cup at a time. Cook for two to three minutes on one side, then flip to cook for the same time on the other.
6. Transfer to an oven-safe plate and place in a warm oven.
7. Drain the dates and press with paper towels to get all the water out. Cut into chunks and put in a blender.
8. Add the pecan butter, one teaspoon vanilla extract and the pinch of sea salt, blending lightly. Add enough water to make a thick but pourable topping.
9. Serve the pancakes with the topping, sprinkled with chopped pecans and shredded coconut on top.

Green With Envy Breakfast Pudding

Chia Seeds Make This Green Pudding Thick And Rich

This breakfast pudding is green because of the spinach, which really doesn't alter the flavor but does give you a great deal of nutritional value. The date is what gives the pudding its sweetness. It tastes more like the almond or coconut milk and the fruit you put on top. The recipe makes one bowl.

Ingredients:
1 Medjool date with pit removed
1 handful fresh spinach
1 cup almond or coconut milk
3 tablespoons chia seeds
Fruit for topping (mango, berries, kiwi, banana)

Directions:
1. Place the pitted date, spinach and milk in a blender and blend until smooth.
2. Pour the blended ingredients into a bowl and add the chia seeds. Stir every few minutes, letting the mixture set for a total of 15 minutes.
3. Cover and refrigerate overnight.
4. Remove from the refrigerator, stir and top with fruit.

Maple Glazed Pumpkin Bread

This is another great quick bread sweetened with bananas and maple syrup. I have included a sweet glaze made with powdered sugar if you desire to use it, but the bread is tasty without anything added. The recipe makes one loaf.

Ingredients:
½ cup plus 2 tablespoons almond milk
1 teaspoon apple cider vinegar
1 banana, mashed
2 cups pumpkin puree (See recipe, Chapter 11.)
3 tablespoons almond butter (See recipe, Chapter 11.)
3 teaspoons vanilla (See recipe, Chapter 11.)
¼ cup maple syrup
¼ teaspoon salt
¾ cup wheat flour
½ cup old-fashioned rolled oats
½ teaspoon baking soda
1½ teaspoons baking powder
½ teaspoon cinnamon
¼ teaspoon nutmeg
⅛ teaspoon ground cloves
¼ cup chopped walnuts

Glaze Ingredients:
6 tablespoons powdered sugar
2 tablespoons maple syrup
¼ teaspoon cinnamon

Directions:
1. Preheat the oven to 350 degrees, Fahrenheit and line the bottom of an oiled loaf pan with a strip of parchment paper, cut long enough to rise above the short sides of the loaf pan.
2. Combine the milk with the vinegar in a small bowl and whisk well. Set the bowl aside for five minutes, until the milk starts to curdle.

109

3. In a large bowl, whisk together the mashed banana, pumpkin puree, almond butter, vanilla and maple syrup.
4. In another bowl, whisk together the salt, flour, rolled oats, baking soda, baking powder, cinnamon, nutmeg and cloves.
5. Add the curdled milk to the mashed banana mixture and combine thoroughly.
6. Gradually add the dry mixture to the wet ingredients, mixing well after each addition until well combined.
7. Mix in the walnuts and pour the batter over the parchment paper in the loaf pan.
8. Bake for 25 minutes or until a toothpick inserted into the center comes out clean. Let the bread cool for 10 minutes while making the glaze.
9. Mix the glaze ingredients together and drizzle over the bread. Let this cool for at least 10 more minutes before slicing.

Mashed Potato Pancakes

These pancakes are a little more refined than latkes, but they taste very similar. Latkes are made with shredded potatoes but these are made with mashed, so the texture is more like a regular pancake. They are super tasty served with sour cream, if you eat dairy. If you don't do dairy, you'll enjoy a topping of applesauce with a little cinnamon and stevia added. It's to die for! This recipe makes enough for four people.

Ingredients:
3 medium potatoes (Russet or Yukon Gold), peeled and sliced
½ to ¾ cup unsweetened soy, almond, or coconut milk
Salt and pepper to taste
1 tablespoon parsley
1 tablespoon chives (optional)
¼ cup whole-wheat flour or rolled oats
¼ cup green onion, chopped
1 tablespoon oil or butter

Directions:

1. Make mashed potatoes first or use leftovers (you'll need about two cups of mashed potatoes). You can make a fresh batch by boiling some potato pieces in enough water to cover them, until they are soft, then draining and mashing them, along with butter and milk, if you eat dairy
2. Add the parsley and chives and hand mix these.
3. Add the flour or rolled oats and beat them in briefly. Don't beat the mixture too much or the pancakes will become sticky and tough. You want the mixture to look like loose mashed potatoes.
4. Stir in the green onion.
5. Heat a large skillet and pour in a little of the oil or butter and let melt. Drop the potato mixture by large spoonfuls and spread them with a spoon. Cook for two to three minutes on each side or until brown. Use more of the oil or butter as needed when making the rest of the pancakes, to prevent them from sticking to the pan.
6. Transfer the pancakes to plates and top with sour cream, applesauce, or even maple syrup.

Eggless Breakfast Tacos

Instead of egg, these tacos are filled with vegetables, mushrooms, potatoes, beans and quinoa for a nutritious and filling breakfast. The recipe makes four to six servings.

Ingredients:
½ onion, diced
1 handful of mushrooms, cleaned and chopped
½ any color bell pepper, seeded and chopped
1 cup cauliflower, cut into florets
1 large baked potato, peeled and diced
1 15.5-ounce can cannellini beans, drained and rinsed
½ cup cooked quinoa
½ teaspoon turmeric
1 teaspoon garlic powder
¼ teaspoon salt
¼ teaspoon pepper
Corn tortillas

Directions:

1. Coat a skillet with nonstick spray or add a teaspoon of canola oil or water and warm it over medium heat.
2. Add the onion, mushroom, bell pepper and cauliflower. Sauté, stirring until the vegetables soften. You'll want to add a little water or canola oil if they start to stick to the pan.
3. Stir in the potato, beans and quinoa; season with turmeric, garlic powder, salt and pepper.
4. Spoon into tortillas, fold and serve.

Oatmeal Bars with Chocolate Chips and Pumpkin Seed

You can Cut Into Squares Instead of Bars

This is another bar recipe that is hard to pass up on a day when you slept in and need to get out the door quick. They also make tasty snacks. Keep the 16 bars in an airtight container and they will last about a week if you don't eat them before then. One ingredient is brown rice syrup and this, plus the maple syrup is what gives the bars their sweetness. Find brown rice syrup at your local health food store.

Ingredients:

1¼ cups oat flour (See recipe, Chapter 11)

1½ cups old-fashioned rolled oats
3½ tablespoons pumpkin seeds
3 tablespoons mini chocolate chips (vegan chocolate chips or raisins instead)
1 teaspoon ground cinnamon
⅛ teaspoon ground nutmeg
¼ teaspoon sea salt
¼ cup plus 2 tablespoon unsweetened coconut milk
2 tablespoons maple syrup
⅓ cup brown rice syrup

Directions:
1. Preheat the oven to 350 degrees, Fahrenheit and line an eight by eight-inch baking dish with parchment paper.
2. In a large bowl, combine the flour, oats, pumpkin seeds, chocolate chips or raisins, cinnamon, nutmeg and salt.
3. In another bowl whisk the milk, maple syrup and rice syrup together.
4. Add the wet ingredients to the dry ingredients and pour the resulting batter into the prepared pan.
5. Make cuts for the bars with a sharp knife before putting into the oven.
6. Bake 20 minutes and let cool in the pan. Use a knife to cut totally through the bars.

Potato Shallot Frittata with Kick

This frittata contains no eggs; instead it uses tofu. The flavor is excellent. You will need a deep dish pie for this one. It makes about eight wedges.

Ingredients:
1 tablespoon water (more if the ingredients stick)
2 cups potatoes (red or Yukon gold), peeled and cut into small cubes
¾ cup shallots, chopped
1¼ cups bell pepper, chopped (any color or combination of colors)
¾ cup unsweetened almond or soy milk

½ cup raw cashews

1 large clove garlic, minced

1 tablespoon fresh squeezed lemon juice

2 teaspoons miso

¼ teaspoon ground mustard

½ teaspoon sea salt

¼ teaspoon ground pepper

¼ teaspoon dill seed

2 teaspoons fresh thyme or oregano, chopped

1 12-ounce package extra firm tofu

¼ cup oat bran or gluten-free bread crumbs

1 pinch more sea salt

Directions:

1. Preheat the oven to 375 degrees, Fahrenheit.
2. In a skillet over medium heat, pour the water and put in the potatoes, shallots, salt and pepper and sauté until cooked through (about 15 to 20 minutes). Keep stirring and add more water if they start to stick.
3. Add the bell peppers and cook through.
4. In a blender, pour the milk, cashews, garlic, lemon juice, miso, mustard, salt and pepper. Pulse and add the thyme and the tofu. Blend until creamy.
5. Remove your vegetables from the skillet to a bowl and pour the ingredients into the blender. If it seems too thick, add a tablespoon or two of milk. Pulse to mix.
6. Pour the mixture into an oiled pie pan and smooth the top.
7. In a small bowl combine the oat bran or bread crumbs with the salt and sprinkle over the top.
8. Bake for 40 to 45 minutes and switch to broil for as long as it takes to brown the top. Let your quiche cool for 10 to 15 minutes before cutting into wedges.

Sweet Potato Breakfast Hash Browns

Did you know that sweet potatoes are supposed to help you lose weight? They are low in calories and high in fiber, so they take up room in your stomach to make you feel full longer. Because fiber digests slower than other foods, you do not feel hungry as quickly. If I could, I would eat this every day, but unfortunately I like diversity. This recipe makes four servings.

Ingredients:
  1 large onion, chopped
  1 large red or green bell pepper, seeded and chopped
  2 large sweet potatoes or yams, peeled and chopped
  ½ teaspoon paprika
  ½ teaspoon salt
  ¼ teaspoon pepper

Directions:
  1. Heat a non-stick skillet over medium heat and sprinkle in some oil or water. Cook the onions until they are translucent.
  2. Add the bell peppers and potatoes and stir to cook. Keep stirring so they don't stick to the pan. Add water if they do start to stick
  3. Once the potatoes are softened to your liking, add the paprika, salt and pepper.

4. Make sure any liquid that may have accumulated is evaporated before you serve it up.

The next chapter will give you all kinds of different ideas on what you can serve for lunch when you eat at home or even when you brown bag it to work or school.

Chapter 5: Lunches You Will Love

Breakfast is important, but so is lunch. It must keep you going strong until dinner, as long as five or six hours away. The lunch selections in this chapter are all plant-based. Some will include dairy products, but not all.

You'll find in this chapter sandwich spreads, pinwheels, wraps and more. Everything here is designed to keep you going strong all afternoon.

I particularly love spreads. You make them up, put them in the refrigerator and take them out to spread on lunch the next day. If you don't want the same flavor every day, you can vary your toppings or use a different kind of bread base. Change things up by topping the spread with some fresh basil, crushed nuts or sunflower seeds. Add cucumber slices, chopped cilantro, or a little celery seed. You can add anything to a wrap, including shredded raw vegetables. Pinwheels introduce some whimsical variety to your meal. They're basically a wrap, sliced crosswise, but the colorful spirals are fun to eat.

Many of the recipes in this chapter call for hummus. While you can buy hummus pre-made, it's simple enough to make for yourself. You'll find a basic hummus recipe in chapter 11 of this book,

You'll also find sun-dried tomatoes among the ingredients in this chapter. I avoid the canned or jarred varieties, because they are preserved in oil. Instead, I get mine in a bag; they actually resemble dehydrated tomatoes. Just soak the tomatoes in water to partially reconstitute them before using. They add a pop of concentrated tomato flavor that I love.

Artichoke White Bean Sandwich Spread

Green Onions Add Color And Flavor To This Dip

This spread is tasty and packs a wallop of protein and fiber. You can spread it on bread, crackers, pita bread, or rolled up inside a wrap. It makes two heaping cups that will keep in the refrigerator for about a week.

Ingredients:

½ cup raw cashews, chopped
Water
1 clove garlic, cut into half
1 tablespoon lemon zest
1 teaspoon fresh rosemary, chopped
¼ teaspoon salt
¼ teaspoon pepper
6 tablespoons almond, soy or coconut milk
1 15.5-ounce can cannellini beans, rinsed and drained well
3 to 4 canned artichoke hearts, chopped
¼ cup hulled sunflower seeds (use raw, roasted, or salted)
Green onions, chopped, for garnish (optional)

Directions:

1. Soak the raw cashews for 15 minutes in enough water to cover them. Drain and dab with a paper towel to make them as dry as possible.

118

2. Transfer the cashews to a blender and add the garlic, lemon zest, rosemary, salt and pepper. Pulse to break everything up and then add the milk, one tablespoon at a time, until the mixture is smooth and creamy. (You may not need the full amount).
3. Mash the beans in a bowl with a fork. Add the artichoke hearts and sunflower seeds. Toss to mix.
4. Pour the cashew mixture on top and season with more salt and pepper if desired. Mix the ingredients well and spread on whole-wheat bread, crackers, or a wrap.

Buffalo Chickpea Wraps

The Lettuce Will Cool Your Mouth Down After The Buffalo Heat

If you like the spicy flavor of "buffalo" this recipe will prove you don't need chicken to enjoy it. Instead, we use chickpeas. There are two parts to this recipe: the buffalo chickpeas – which are fine for snacking on, all by themselves – and the salad. Combined in a wrap, they create a genuine taste sensation. The recipe serves four people.

Ingredients:
¼ cup plus 2 tablespoons hummus (See chapter 11 for the recipe)
2 tablespoons lemon juice
1½ tablespoons maple syrup

1 to 2 tablespoons hot water

1 head Romaine lettuce, chopped

1 15-ounce can chickpeas, drained, rinsed and patted dry

4 tablespoons hot sauce, divided (less if desired) (See recipe, Chapter 11.)

1 tablespoon olive or coconut oil)

¼ teaspoon garlic powder

1 pinch sea salt

4 wheat tortillas

¼ cup cherry tomatoes, diced (See recipe, Chapter 11.)

¼ cup red onion, diced

¼ of a ripe avocado (optional), thinly sliced

Directions:

1. Mix the hummus with the lemon juice and maple syrup in a large bowl. Use a whisk and add the hot water, a little at a time until it is thick but spreadable.
2. Add the Romaine lettuce and toss to coat. Set aside.
3. Pour the prepared chickpeas into another bowl. Add three tablespoons of the hot sauce, the olive oil, garlic powder and salt; toss to coat.
4. Heat a metal skillet (cast iron works the best) over medium heat and add the chickpea mixture. Sauté for three to five minutes and mash gently with a spoon.
5. Once the chickpea mixture is slightly dried out, remove from the heat and add the rest of the hot sauce. Stir it in well and set aside.
6. Lay the tortillas on a clean, flat surface and spread a quarter cup of the buffalo chickpeas on top. Top with tomatoes, onion and avocado (optional) and wrap.

Coconut Veggie Wraps

Coconut wraps can be found at whole food stores in a variety of flavors. I particularly like the wrap flavored with turmeric. Pick your favorite and try it.

You can make this wrap for lunch or use it as an appetizer for a party. The recipe yields five wraps.

Ingredients:

- 1½ cups shredded carrots
- 1 red bell pepper, seeded and thinly sliced
- 2½ cups kale (or baby spinach if you don't like kale)
- 1 ripe avocado, thinly sliced
- 1 cup fresh cilantro, chopped
- 5 coconut wraps
- ⅔ cups hummus
- 6½ cups green curry paste (See chapter 11 for the recipe)

Directions:

1. Slice, chop and shred all the vegetables.
2. Lay a coconut wrap on a clean flat surface and spread two tablespoons of the hummus and one tablespoon of the green curry paste on top of the end closest to you.
3. Place some carrots, bell pepper, kale and cilantro on the wrap and start rolling it up, starting from the edge closest to you. Roll tightly and fold in the ends.
4. Place the wrap, seam down, on a plate to serve.

Cucumber Avocado Sandwich

Homemade Whole Wheat Bread Makes A Delicious Sandwich

This sandwich is fresh and tasty. You can omit the avocado, if you prefer and double the slices of cucumber for an even fresher treat. Cucumber tends to be a little watery but here is a trick to make it a little drier. I would not advise taking this as a brown bag lunch because sitting cucumbers will start to get soggy no matter what you do. Instead, make them for a weekend treat or take all the ingredients to work and slice the cucumber there. This recipe makes two sandwiches.

Ingredients:
½ of a large cucumber, peeled and sliced
¼ teaspoon salt
4 slices whole-wheat bread
4 ounces goat cheese with or without herbs, at room temperature
2 Romaine lettuce leaves
1 large avocado, peeled, pitted and sliced
2 pinches lemon pepper
1 squeeze of lemon juice
½ cup alfalfa sprouts

Directions:
1. Peel and slice the cucumber thinly. Lay the slices on a plate and sprinkle them with a quarter to a half teaspoon of salt. Let this set for 10 minutes or until water appears on the plate.
2. Place the cucumber slices in a colander and rinse with cold water. Let this drain, then place on a dry plate and pat dry with a paper towel.
3. Spread all slices with goat cheese and place lettuce leaves on the two bottom pieces of bread.
4. Layer the cucumber slices and avocado atop the bread.
5. Sprinkle one pinch of lemon pepper over each sandwich and drizzle a little lemon juice over the top.
6. Top with the alfalfa sprouts and place another piece of bread, goat cheese down, on top.

Lentil Sandwich Spread

Lentils bear a delicious, earthy flavor. You can use either green or red lentils for this spread and add lettuce, spinach, basil leaves, mint leaves or watercress if you wish, for a bit of variety. The recipe makes two cups and it keeps well in the refrigerator for about a week.

Ingredients:
- 1 tablespoon water or oil
- 1 small onion, chopped
- 2 cloves garlic, minced
- 1 cup dry lentils
- 2 cups vegetable stock (See recipe, Chapter 11.)
- 1 tablespoon apple cider vinegar
- 2 tablespoons tomato paste
- 3 sun-dried tomatoes
- 2 tablespoons maple or agave syrup
- 1 teaspoon dried oregano
- ½ teaspoon ground cumin
- 1 teaspoon coriander
- 1 teaspoon turmeric
- ½ lemon, juiced
- 1 tablespoon fresh parsley, chopped

Directions:
1. Warm a Dutch oven over medium heat and add the water or oil.
2. Immediately add the onions and sauté for two to three minutes or until softened. Add more water if this starts to stick to the pan.
3. Add the garlic and sauté for one minute.
4. Add the lentils, vegetable stock and vinegar; bring to a boil. Turn down to a simmer and cook for 15 minutes or until the lentils are soft and the liquid is almost completely absorbed.
5. Ladle the lentils into a food processor and add the tomato paste, sun-dried tomatoes and syrup; process until smooth.

6. Add the oregano, cumin, coriander, turmeric and lemon; processes until thoroughly mixed.
7. Remove the spread to a bowl and apply it to bread, toast, a wrap, or pita. Sprinkle With toppings as desired.

Mediterranean Tortilla Pinwheels

If you like Mediterranean flavors such as olives, tomatoes and artichokes, you will enjoy taking a few of these pinwheels to work and making your co-workers drool. You can use black olives if you wish, but I prefer to slice whole pimento-stuffed green olives. This recipe will give you four or five tortilla rolls that you then cut into pinwheels. You'll want to make these as you need them, since they look and taste best when fresh. I store the rest of the sauce in the refrigerator. You can also use the sauce as a salad dressing, if you wish.

Ingredients:
½ cup water
4 tablespoons white vinegar
3 tablespoons lemon juice
3 tablespoons tahini paste
1 clove garlic, minced
Salt and pepper to taste
Canned artichokes, drained and thinly sliced
Cherry tomatoes, thinly sliced
Olives, thinly sliced
Lettuce or baby spinach
Tortillas

Directions:
1. In a bowl, combine the water, vinegar, lemon juice and Tahini paste; whisk together until smooth.
2. Add the garlic, salt and pepper to taste; whisk to combine. Set the bowl aside.
3. Lay a tortilla on a flat surface and spread with one tablespoon of the sauce.
4. Lay some lettuce or spinach slices on top, then scatter some artichoke, tomato and olive slices on top.

5. Tightly roll the tortilla and fold in the sides. Cut the ends off and then slice into four or five pinwheels.

Pita Pizza

Pita Bread Makes A Perfect Pizza Base

I still get cravings for pizza. Even though I do cheat sometimes, this pita pizza is a pretty good alternative and it's easy to make. Kids love it, even with all the vegetables on top. I am not giving any measurements for the pizza toppings because the quantities all depend on your preferences; mix or match to your own delight. This makes one pizza.

Ingredients:
1 pita
Hummus (See recipe, Chapter 11.)
Marinara sauce (See recipe, Chapter 11.)
Various chopped vegetables (onions, cauliflower, broccoli, mushrooms etc.)
Shredded cheese (regular or vegan)

Directions:
1. Preheat the oven to 350 degrees, Fahrenheit.
2. Place the pita bread on a baking pan coated with nonstick spray.
3. Spread the pita with hummus and then spoon on a light layer of marinara sauce.
4. Lay down your vegetables on top and sprinkle with cheese.

5. Bake for five to 10 minutes until everything is hot and bubbly.

Rice and Bean Burritos

This recipe makes six burritos that are great for lunch get-togethers. They are just rice and beans inside a tortilla, but sometimes the most simple can be the most delicious. Make guacamole or salsa for serving. These burritos are easily frozen; just take out and thaw before baking, any time you need them. I usually keep some made up in my freezer, just in case.

Ingredients:
2 16-ounce cans fat-free refried beans (See recipe, Chapter 11.)
6 tortillas (I use wheat or flour, but you can also use gluten-free)
2 cups cooked rice
½ cup salsa (See recipe, Chapter 11.)
1 tablespoon olive oil
1 bunch green onions, chopped
2 bell peppers, finely chopped
Guacamole

Directions:
1. Preheat the oven to 375 degrees, Fahrenheit.
2. Dump the refried beans into a saucepan and place over medium heat to warm.
3. Heat the tortillas and lay them out on a flat surface.
4. Spoon the beans in a long mound that runs across the tortilla, just a little off from center.
5. Spoon some rice and salsa over the beans; add the green pepper and onions to taste, along with any other finely chopped vegetables you like.
6. Fold over the shortest edge of plain tortilla and roll it up, folding in the sides as you go.
7. Place each burrito, seam side down, on a nonstick-sprayed baking sheet.
8. Brush with olive oil and bake for 15 minutes.

9. Serve with guacamole.

Ricotta Basil Pinwheels

Basil Pinwheels Are Refreshingly Flavorful

This recipe says "ricotta" but it is more "ricotta-like," because it is made using tofu instead of cheese. Yes, it's another pinwheel recipe, but the fresh flavor of basil leaves adds refreshing flavor.

The ricotta replacement is made using cashews and tofu; it has the texture of regular dairy ricotta cheese. The cashews are soaked, making them easier to run through a blender, but if you have a high-speed blender, you can skip the soaking if you wish.

I use wheat tortillas, but you can also use corn or gluten free. Finally, you don't have to cut them into pinwheels if you don't want to. Just eat them like a wrap. The pinwheels just look prettier.

Ingredients:
½ cup unsalted cashews
Water
7 ounces (1 block) firm tofu, cut into pieces
¼ cup almond milk
1 teaspoon white wine vinegar
1 clove garlic, smashed

127

20 to 25 fresh basil leaves
Salt and pepper to taste
8 tortillas
7 ounces fresh spinach
½ cup black olives, sliced
2 to 3 tomatoes, cut into small pieces

Directions:

1. Soak the cashews for 30 minutes in enough water to cover them. Drain them well and pat them dry with paper towels.
2. Place the cashews in a blender along with the tofu, almond milk, vinegar, garlic, basil leaves, salt and pepper to taste. Blend until smooth and creamy.
3. Spread the resulting mixture on the eight tortillas, dividing it equally.
4. Top with spinach leaves, olives and tomatoes.
5. Tightly roll each loaded tortilla.
6. Cut off the ends with a sharp knife and slice into four or five pinwheels.

Sloppy Joes Made with Lentils and Bulgur

Delicious Sloppy Joes With No Meat

This meatless sloppy Joe recipe tastes much like what I remember eating as a kid, only it was made out of hamburger. I use red lentils because they more closely resemble meat; they also hold up well to the cooking. This recipe makes enough for six sandwiches.

Ingredients:

5 tablespoons vegetable stock (See recipe, Chapter 11.)
2 stalks celery, diced
1 small onion, diced
1 small red bell pepper, diced
1 teaspoon garlic powder
1 teaspoon chili powder
1 teaspoon ground cumin
1 teaspoon salt
1 cup cooked bulgur wheat
1 cup red lentils
1 15-ounce can tomato sauce
4 tablespoons tomato paste
3½ cups water
2 teaspoons balsamic vinegar
1 tablespoon Hoisin sauce

Directions:

1. In a Dutch oven, heat up the vegetable stock and add the celery, onion and bell pepper. Sauté until vegetables are soft, about five minutes.
2. Add the garlic powder, chili powder, cumin and salt and mix in.
3. Add the bulgur wheat, lentils, tomato sauce, tomato paste, water, vinegar and Hoisin sauce. Stir and bring to a boil.
4. Turn the heat down to a simmer and cook uncovered for 30 minutes. Stir occasionally to prevent sticking and scorching.
5. Taste to see if the lentils are tender.
6. When the lentils are done, serve on buns.

Spicy Hummus and Apple Wrap

Hummus and apples are a treat in my house. I like to take apple slices soaked in lemon juice and dip them in hummus. That can make a delicious part of a good plant-based lunch, but when combined in a wrap, you've got something truly delightful! This recipe calls for a bag of broccoli slaw; you can find this in most grocery stores, right along with the pre-cut cabbage slaw. This recipe makes a single wrap.

Ingredients:
3 to 4 tablespoons hummus
2 tablespoons mild salsa (optional) (See recipe, Chapter 11.)
½ cup broccoli slaw
½ teaspoon fresh lemon juice
2 teaspoons plain yogurt or vegan yogurt
salt and pepper to taste
1 tortilla
Lettuce leaves
½ Granny Smith or other tart apple, cored and thinly sliced

Directions:
1. In a small bowl, mix the hummus with the salsa. Set the bowl aside.
2. In a large bowl, mix the broccoli slaw, lemon juice and yogurt. Season with the salt and pepper.
3. Lay the tortilla on a flat surface and spread on the hummus mixture.
4. Lay down some lettuce leaves on top of the hummus.
5. On the upper half of the tortilla, place a pile of the broccoli slaw mixture and cover with the apples.
6. Fold and wrap.

Sun-dried Tomato Spread

Sun-dried Tomatoes Look Ugly, But They Pack Great Flavor

This spread is delicious on wheat bread or toast or just as a dip for wheat crackers. Do not use sun-dried tomatoes in a jar because they are packed with oil. Get the unadulterated dehydrated tomatoes. This makes about two cups of spread and keeps in the refrigerator for about a week.

Ingredients:
    1 cup sun-dried tomatoes
    1 cup raw cashews
    Water for soaking tomatoes and cashews
    ½ cup water
    1 clove garlic, minced
    1 green onion, chopped
    5 large basil leaves
    ½ teaspoon lemon juice
    ¼ teaspoon salt
    1 dash pepper
    Hulled sunflower seeds (salted or unsalted)

Directions:

1. Soak tomatoes and cashews for 30 minutes in separate bowls, with enough water to cover them. Drain and pat dry.
2. Put the tomatoes and cashews in a food processor and puree them, drizzling the water in as it purees to make a smooth, creamy paste.
3. Add the garlic, onion, basil leaves, lemon juice, salt and pepper and mix thoroughly.
4. Scrape into a bowl, cover and refrigerate overnight.
5. Spread on bread or toast and sprinkle with sunflower seeds for a little added crunch.

Sweet Potato Sandwich Spread

Try Spreading Sweet Potato Spread On Top With Vegetables

Any leftovers of this spread will not last long, but it will keep for about a week in the refrigerator. It is sweet and creamy and bright orange in color. This recipe makes enough for a large sandwich.

Ingredients:
1 large sweet potato baked and peeled

1 teaspoon cumin

1 teaspoon chili powder

1 teaspoon garlic powder

Salt and pepper to taste

2 slices whole-wheat bread

1 to 2 tablespoons pinto beans or black beans, drained

Lettuce

Directions:

1. Bake and peel the sweet potato and mash it in a bowl. If it is too thick, add a little almond or coconut milk.
2. Mix in the cumin, chili powder, garlic powder, salt and pepper.
3. Spread the mixture on a slice of bread and spoon some beans on top.
4. Top with lettuce leaves and the other slice of bread.

Zucchini Sandwich with Balsamic Dressing

This tasty sandwich is made with zucchini slices and that are cooked in a skillet with a lovely balsamic dressing on top. The recipe makes two sandwiches. Note: if you won't be eating the sandwich immediately, wait until you're ready to eat before adding the dressing.

Ingredients:

2 small zucchinis, cut lengthwise into half-inch thick strips

1 tablespoon olive oil

4 cloves garlic, thinly sliced

1 tablespoon balsamic vinegar

1 large roasted red pepper, chopped

1 cup cannellini beans, rinsed and drained

2 whole-wheat sandwich rolls or bread

6 to 8 basil leaves

½ teaspoon pepper

Directions:

1. Add the oil to a hot skillet and sauté the garlic for one or two minutes or until it just starts to brown.

2. Add the zucchini strips and sauté in batches (don't overcrowd) and lay out on a plate until they are all finished.
3. Reduce heat to medium and place all the zucchini strips back in the pan.
4. Add the vinegar and sauté for about a minute.
5. In the blender, process the red pepper and beans until smooth.
6. Toast the buns and spoon onto the bottom halves the bean and pepper mixture.
7. Lay basil leaves on top and then the zucchini.
8. Grind some pepper on top and close the sandwich with the top of the bun.

The next chapter will give you some salads that can also make a great lunch. Some of these salads are also suitable for dinner.

Chapter 6: Salads Done Right

This chapter contains a bunch of salads that are all plant-based. Some involve greens, others fruit; still more of these salads call for pasta or potatoes. Here you'll find some unusual titles, like the Watermelon Blackberry Caprese salad. You'll also find some old faithfuls, such as Four Bean Salad. You have plenty of variety here from which to choose; they all make great sides, lunches or main dishes.

Apple Mint Salad With Pine Nut Crunch

Pomegranate Fruit Is The Seed; Tastes Great With Apples & Mint

The flavor of apples with mint is truly refreshing and then you add the crunch of pine nuts. Start by soaking apple slices in lemon juice so they do not turn brown and add the sweetness of maple syrup. You can garnish this salad with fresh mint, but you must use the dried leaves for the right flavor. To dry mint place a few sprigs in a brown paper lunch bag and catch the ends of the stems in the open end of the bag crunching it all down around them. Secure with a little string and hang from a nail so that the bag is suspended in the air in a warm area that does not receive a great deal of sun. The attic of my old house was a favorite drying place, but with no attic, I hang them from the rafters of my garage. The

135

bag keeps dust out. This recipe makes one salad, so double it for two.

Ingredients:
1 medium apple, diced (I use a tart apple like Granny Smith, or Cortland)
1 tablespoon lemon juice
1 teaspoon maple syrup (try agave syrup for another flavor)
½ teaspoon dried mint
1 tablespoon fresh pomegranate seeds
1 teaspoon pine nuts or sliced almonds

Directions:
1. Toast the nuts in a pan on the stove. Stir constantly so they don't burn and let them turn a golden brown. Set the pan aside until cooled to room temperature.
2. Place the diced apple in a small bowl with the lemon juice and stir around so all the apple is coated.
3. Add the maple syrup and dried mint and stir it in.
4. Sprinkle the top of the salad with pomegranate seeds and toasted nuts.

Chickpea 'N Spinach Tomato Salad

The chickpeas give protein power to this salad made with tender baby spinach leaves. The sesame and flaxseed give it a little crunch and this recipe makes two servings.

Ingredients:
2 cups canned or cooked chickpeas
4 medium tomatoes, chopped (I like Roma tomatoes)
5 green onions, chopped (use the white and part of the green sections)
1 red bell pepper, seeded and chopped
⅓ cup fresh parsley, chopped
1 cup baby spinach leaves
2 tablespoons olive oil
½ lemon, juiced
1 tablespoon balsamic vinegar

2 tablespoons flaxseed
2 tablespoons sesame seeds

Directions:

1. Combine the chickpeas, tomatoes, onion, bell pepper, parsley and baby spinach in a large salad bowl.
2. In a jar with a lid, combine the oil, lemon juice and balsamic vinegar; shake until well mixed.
3. Pour the dressing over the salad and sprinkle with the flaxseed and sesame seeds.

Fennel Chickpea Salad with Quinoa

The Bulb That Grows Underground Is The Part Used In This Salad

Quinoa makes for a filling salad and it is considered a superfood. You can't go wrong with quinoa. You want the flavor of the fennel and vegetables to come through, so I use white quinoa and rinse it well to get rid of any impurities. Other quinoas have a stronger flavor. This recipe yields four to six servings.

Ingredients:

½ cup uncooked quinoa, rinsed
1¼ cups water

¼ teaspoon sea salt

1½ cups fennel bulb, sliced as thinly as possible

2 cups baby arugula or spinach

1 cup canned chickpeas

¼ cup radishes, thinly sliced

1 cup cherry tomatoes, halved

¼ cup green onions, chopped

1 tablespoon water

2 tablespoons fresh lemon juice

½ teaspoon lemon zest

½ tablespoon fresh mint leaves, minced

1 tablespoon fresh parsley, minced

1 teaspoon Dijon mustard

½ teaspoon agave nectar

¼ teaspoon sea salt

⅛ teaspoon pepper

Directions:

1. Pour the uncooked quinoa, water and a quarter teaspoon of salt into a saucepan over medium heat. Let it come to a boil, then reduce to a simmer, cover and let it cook for 15 to 20 minutes or until the quinoa is cooked and the liquid is all absorbed.
2. Fluff the quinoa with a fork and place in a bowl. Refrigerate, uncovered, for 15 minutes.
3. Place the cooled quinoa in a large salad bowl and add the fennel, arugula or spinach, chickpeas, radishes, tomatoes and green onion, tossing to combine.
4. In a small bowl, combine the water, lemon juice, lemon zest, mint, parsley, mustard, agave nectar, sea salt and pepper; whisk together thoroughly.
5. Pour this dressing over the salad and toss until everything is coated. Refrigerate for 15 to 20 minutes before serving.

Mango and Red Cabbage Slaw

This Slaw Is Almost Too Pretty To Eat, But Not After You Taste It

I like coleslaw, but it can be boringly similar. *This* slaw recipe, however, is anything *but* boring. The red cabbage and golden mango combine to give you a flavor you won't soon forget. You'll find it a feast for the eyes as well, with its combination of golden mango, orange carrot, red cabbage and green cilantro. You may just choose never to eat that old boring coleslaw again. This recipe makes four servings.

Ingredients:
2 ripe mangos, sliced
¼ cup fresh cilantro, chopped
4 carrots, peeled and grated
4 cups red cabbage, shredded
1 splash of balsamic vinegar
1 lime, juiced
1 pinch kosher salt

Directions:
1. Place the mango, cilantro, carrot and red cabbage in a large salad bowl.
2. Whisk together in another bowl the vinegar, lime juice and salt.
3. Pour the dressing over the salad and toss to coat.

4. For the most refreshing flavor, refrigerate for 20 minutes before serving.

Maple Carrot Salad Delight

Maple Carrot Salad's Sweetness And Crunch Make It Fun To Eat

Maple syrup brings this salad to life, adding to the natural sweetness of the carrots. The salad is further enhanced by the walnuts and raisins. This recipe makes four servings that are irresistible to both adults and children.

Ingredients:
1½ cups fresh grated or shredded carrots
⅔ cups raisins (I use golden raisins to further enhance the sweetness)
¾ cup walnuts, chopped (or pecans, almonds or sunflower seeds)
4 tablespoons maple syrup
⅛ teaspoon sea salt

Directions:

1. In a bowl, combine the carrots, raisins, nuts, syrup and salt, mixing well.
2. Chill, covered, for at least three hours, if not overnight.
3. Serve while cold.

New Four Bean Salad

Stir In Some Wax Beans To Make It A Five Bean Salad

My grandmother used to take this to church and neighborhood potlucks. I hated it as a child, but once I became older and my taste buds settled down a bit, it became a standard favorite in my home. The four beans are cannellini beans, canned green beans, kidney beans and garbanzo beans (chickpeas), but you can combine any beans you like. This recipe makes six to eight servings.

Ingredients:

1 15-ounce can cannellini beans, rinsed and drained
1 15-ounce can green beans, rinsed and drained
1 15-ounce can dark kidney beans, rinsed and drained
1 15-ounce can garbanzo beans, rinsed and drained
2 cups frozen and thawed corn kernels, drained
½ cup red onion, finely chopped
1 large red bell pepper, diced
1 lemon juiced

¼ cup apple cider vinegar (for a change, use rice vinegar or white wine vinegar)
1 teaspoon ground coriander
2 teaspoons ground cumin
⅛ teaspoon cayenne pepper (adjust to taste)

Directions:

1. Drain and rinse all the beans together, then pour into a large bowl.
2. Add the corn, onion and bell pepper; stir to mix.
3. In a small bowl, whisk together the lemon juice, vinegar, coriander, cumin and cayenne pepper. Pour over the beans and toss well.
4. Chill for at least two hours before serving. It tastes even better if you let it chill overnight.

Orangey Almond Salad

This salad has great flavor and will wake up those taste buds. It has the sweetness and tartness of oranges and dried cranberries mixed with the herbal flavor of the parsley. The dressing of vinegar, maple syrup and garlic blends sweet and sour in a complementary combination that sets off well the other flavors. This recipe makes enough for four people.

Ingredients:

½ cup slivered almonds
⅓ cup dried cranberries
½ cup green onions, diced
⅓ cup parsley, chopped
1 head romaine lettuce, torn into small pieces
1 can mandarin oranges, drained
1 clove garlic, minced
¼ cup apple cider vinegar
1 tablespoon olive oil
2 tablespoons maple syrup
Salt and pepper to taste

Directions:

1. Place the almonds, cranberries, parsley, green onions and romaine lettuce in a large salad bowl.
2. Add the drained mandarin oranges and toss to combine.
3. In a small bowl, whisk together the garlic, vinegar, oil and maple syrup. Season with salt and pepper.
4. Pour over the salad, toss and serve.

Peanut-Dressed Asian Salad

Make Dressing To Use With Carrots, Cabbage & Bell Pepper

I love peanut flavor, so I'm very grateful I'm not allergic to the nuts in this dressing. This salad is great for any luncheon; you're sure to get raves over it.

Ingredients:
3 tablespoons sesame, toasted and divided
3 tablespoons toasted sesame oil
2 tablespoons soy sauce (See recipe, Chapter 11.)
1 tablespoon honey
¼ cup rice wine vinegar
¼ cup vegetable oil
3 tablespoons creamy peanut butter (See recipe, Chapter 11.)
1 teaspoon fresh ginger, peeled and chopped
½ pound sugar snap peas
6 cups baby spinach
¼ red onion, thinly sliced

1 red bell pepper, thinly sliced
1 large carrot, grated
½ large cucumber, thinly sliced
½ cup roasted peanuts, chopped

Directions:

1. Lightly toast the sesame seeds over medium heat in a skillet, then set aside.
2. In a bowl, whisk together the sesame oil, soy sauce, honey, vinegar, vegetable oil, peanut butter, ginger and two tablespoons of the toasted sesame seeds.
3. Bring a pot of water to a boil and add the peas. Boil for five minutes, then rinse in cold water and drain well.
4. Combine the spinach, onions, bell pepper, carrot, cucumber and cooled peas in a large bowl.
5. Pour the dressing over the salad and toss to coat. Sprinkle with the remaining sesame seeds and season to taste with salt and pepper.

Plant-based Taco Salad

I'm a real fan of taco salad, but I'm used to it having meat. However, I don't miss the meat at all in this recipe. and use all black beans. You also don't use taco chips. Instead, the recipe includes directions on how to prepare crunchy chickpeas to top the salad; I find them way better than taco chips. I'll often prepare just the chickpeas and eat them by themselves as a snack. This recipe yields four individual bowls of taco salad.

Ingredients:

1 15-ounce can chickpeas, rinsed, drained and dried well in a paper towel
2 teaspoon cumin, divided
2 teaspoons chili powder, divided
½ teaspoon sea salt, divided
¼ teaspoon ground cinnamon
1 15-ounce can black beans, rinsed and drained
½ teaspoon garlic powder
½ teaspoon paprika

½ teaspoon cayenne
¼ cup water
1 head Romaine lettuce, chopped
1 red bell pepper, diced
1 tomato, chopped
1 cup frozen corn kernels, thawed, drained and patted dried
1 avocado, diced (optional)
Creamy Ranch Dressing (Recipe found in Chapter 11)

Directions:

1. Preheat the oven to 400 degrees, Fahrenheit and prepare a lipped baking sheet by covering the surface with parchment paper.
2. In a bowl, sprinkle the drained chickpeas with one teaspoon of the cumin, one teaspoon of the chili powder, a quarter teaspoon of the sea salt and the cinnamon. Toss to coat.
3. Pour this mixture onto the prepared baking sheet, spreading the chickpeas in a single layer. Bake for 10 minutes. Shake the pan to turn over the chickpeas and bake for another 10 minutes. Remove from the oven and let cool.
4. Toss the black beans with the remaining garlic powder and salt, the paprika and the cayenne pepper; pour into a skillet over medium heat. Add the water and stir, cooking for five to six minutes, until warmed through. Set the pan aside.
5. In a large bowl, toss the lettuce, bell pepper, tomatoes, corn and avocado.
6. Place the lettuce in four separate bowls. Spoon the warm black bean mixture on top and sprinkle with the chickpeas.
7. Drizzle on top as much dressing as you please and stir it in.

Plant-Power Chopped Salad

The More Different Vegetables, The Tastier Your Salad Will Be

This salad is full of great tasting vegetables and it is incredibly easy to make. You can use it as a side dish or with some white bean chili. The recipe serves four people.

Ingredients:

1 large head of Romaine lettuce, washed and chopped
2 cups baby arugula, chopped
1 medium zucchini, ends cut off and cut into slices
1 14-ounce can artichoke hearts, drained, dried and chopped
1 14-ounce can chickpeas, rinsed, drained and dried
2 medium carrots, peeled, quartered lengthwise and thinly sliced
¾ cup tomatoes, diced (See recipe, Chapter 11.)
salt and pepper as desired
4 tablespoons shelled sunflower seeds

Directions:

1. Place the chopped lettuce in a large salad bowl; add the arugula and toss to mix.
2. Add the zucchini, artichoke hearts, chickpeas, carrots and tomatoes; toss to combine.
3. Add salt and pepper to your liking and sprinkle the top with sunflower seeds.

4. Serve with creamy ranch dressing (the recipe is in Chapter 11).

Roasted Potato Salad with Pesto

In this recipe you roast the potatoes first and then add a pesto to them. It is different from any potato salad I have ever tasted and it is delicious. You only use a portion of the pesto sauce for the salad, so store the rest in a jar and you can use it as salad dressing, with pasta, or as a sandwich spread. This recipe makes five servings.

Ingredients:
2½ cups red potatoes, cut into halves or quarters (bite-sized pieces)
1 to 2 pinches sea salt
1 pinch black pepper
1 cup chopped walnuts, divided
2 cloves garlic, minced
½ cup (packed) fresh basil leaves
1 avocado, chopped
3 tablespoons lemon (half a lemon)
2 splashes of hot sauce (See recipe, Chapter 11.)
1 red onion, chopped
2 tablespoons fresh chives, chopped

Directions:
1. Preheat the oven to 450 degrees, Fahrenheit and prepare a lipped baking sheet with a piece of parchment paper.
2. Bring a large pot of water to a boil, then add the potatoes and cook for five to eight minutes, until the potatoes are semi-soft when poked with a fork. Drain and rinse with cold water to arrest the cooking process.
3. Spread the potatoes out on the baking pan, sprinkling them with salt and pepper. Put the potatoes in the oven to roast for eight to 12 minutes, until they turn golden brown. Remove the pan from the oven and set aside.
4. Have another pan prepared with parchment paper and spread out the walnuts across it. Reduce the oven

147

temperature to 350 degrees, Fahrenheit and insert the walnuts for four minutes; toss and return them to the oven for another four minutes. Watch them carefully to prevent burning. Remove the nuts from the oven and set aside.

5. Take a half cup of the walnuts and put it in a blender. Pulse to break up the nuts, then add the garlic, basil leaves, avocado, lemon juice and hot sauce. Blend until creamy.
6. Place the potatoes in a large bowl and add the red onions, the chives and rest of the walnuts. Pour a fourth of the pesto onto the mixture and stir it in.
7. Garnish with extra chives and serve.

Southwestern Salad with Black Bean Dressing

Black Beans Stand Out Visually And Add An Earthy Flavor

This salad gives you a taste of the old Southwest. Omit the corn if you can't digest it well; and you can also reduce the jalapenos for a tamer flavor. This is a pasta salad, so if you're eating gluten-free be careful that your pasta contains no gluten. It makes four servings.

Ingredients:
6 ounces elbow macaroni, gluten free or whole-wheat
1 15-ounce can black beans, rinsed and drained, divided
½ cup frozen corn, thawed and drained

1 cup tomatoes, chopped
½ cup red onion, chopped
½ cup red or green bell pepper, chopped
½ of a hot green chili, seeded and finely chopped
¼ cup fresh cilantro, chopped and divided
salt and pepper to taste
3 to 4 tablespoons soy milk (or coconut milk)
½ teaspoon crushed red pepper flakes
1 teaspoon garlic powder
½ teaspoon onion powder
1 teaspoon cumin
½ teaspoon ground mustard (dry mustard)
¼ teaspoon turmeric (optional)
½ teaspoon paprika
½ teaspoon sea salt
2 tablespoons jalapeno pepper, finely chopped
½ teaspoon vinegar
2 tablespoons lime juice

Directions:

1. Cook the pasta per the package directions and drain, then set the pasta aside to cool.
2. Remove ⅓ cup of the black beans that are rinsed and draining and set them aside.
3. In a large bowl, combine the rest of the black beans, half of the cilantro, the corn kernels, tomato, onion, bell pepper, green chili, salt and pepper to taste.
4. In another large bowl combine the remaining portion of black beans and the milk. Mash them together.
5. Add the red pepper flakes, garlic powder, onion powder, cumin, mustard, turmeric, paprika, salt, jalapeno pepper, vinegar and lime juice and whisk all together.
6. Add the drained pasta to the bowl of black beans and pour the dressing over the top.
7. Serve, garnished with the rest of the cilantro.

Strawberry Spinach Salad

Strawberry Spinach Salad Makes A Refreshing Summer Treat

I use spinach in this salad, but kale works nicely, too. The dressing tastes delicious with the strawberries, making it simultaneously tart and sweet. The dried herbs lend luscious flavor to this salad. If you are inclined, toss in a few blueberries as well; they add both color and flavor and complement the rest of the ingredients. This recipe makes two servings of salad.

Ingredients:

2 cups baby spinach, packed
1 cup strawberries, sliced
¼ cup almond slivers
1 teaspoon lemon juice
1 teaspoon soy sauce (See recipe, Chapter 11.)
1 teaspoon olive oil
¼ teaspoon balsamic vinegar
1 pinch dried oregano
1 pinch dried thyme
1 pinch dried sage
1 pinch ground black pepper
1 pinch sea salt

Directions:

1. Combine the spinach and strawberries in a large salad bowl.

2. Sprinkle the almonds on top.
3. In a small bowl, whisk the lemon juice, soy sauce, olive oil, vinegar, oregano, thyme, sage, pepper and salt and whisk vigorously.
4. Pour the dressing over the salad, toss and serve.

Watermelon and Blackberry "Caprese" Salad

For A Refreshing Flavor, Substitute Mint For The Basil

Caprese salad is usually made with tomatoes, basil and mozzarella cheese, but this one uses fruit that color-matches the tomatoes and balances the flavors of the other ingredients. The combination surprised me, but the taste was marvelous. Note: If you can't get blackberries, try using blueberries or raspberries instead

This recipe requires the basil leaves to be rolled up and sliced. To accomplish this, you'll take some of the leaves and stack them. Roll them up from base to tip, then take a sharp knife and thinly slice the roll to create ribbons of basil.

Since my diet is not completely plant-based, I use regular mozzarella cheese, but you can also use vegan cheese. (You can make your own, using the recipe found in Chapter 11.) This recipe makes enough for six servings.

Ingredients:

3 cups watermelon, cut into bite-sized pieces
12 ounces blackberries (You can use frozen berries, but fresh is always best.)
1 cup mozzarella cheese, cut into bite-sized pieces
1 cup fresh basil leaves, rolled and sliced.
3 tablespoons lemon juice
1 tablespoon olive oil
Salt and pepper to taste

Directions:

1. In a large bowl, combine the watermelon, blackberries, mozzarella and basil. Mix gently with your hands.
2. In a small bowl, whisk together the lemon juice, olive oil and salt and pepper.
3. Drizzle the dressing over the salad and toss lightly.

Sweet Broccoli Asparagus Salad with Pecans

Everything in this salad is raw, even the asparagus. I have never eaten fresh asparagus raw before making this salad; now I often add it to my salads. I also include it with raw vegetables for dipping.

This salad is sweet and tart with both vegetables and fruit involved. It makes four servings.

Ingredients:

1 bunch asparagus, cut into 1½-inch pieces
2 medium heads of broccoli, cut into florets
3 cups red grapes, whole or cut in half
3 green onions, sliced
½ cup raw pecans, chopped
¼ cup lemon juice
1 tablespoon lemon zest
2 tablespoons maple or agave syrup
½ cup pecan butter
¼ cup water
Sea salt to taste

Directions:

1. Combine the asparagus, broccoli, grapes, onions and pecans in a large salad bowl and toss.
2. In another bowl, whisk together the lemon juice, lemon zest, syrup, pecan butter and water until smooth and creamy. Season with salt to taste
3. Pour the dressing over the asparagus mixture and toss to coat.

In the next chapter we'll make a whole range of soups and stews that are all plant-based. We'll use all sorts of vegetables, different beans and grains and sometimes even a little tofu.

Chapter 7: World Class Soups And Stews

Soups and stews are part of the fabric of life. Even when there's little to eat, there's always a way to stretch the food by making soup.

Remember the old story of "Stone Soup?" A soldier walks into town and tells the villagers that he has some wonderful stones with which to make soup; all he needs is just a bit of vegetables and some meat to make it wonderful. He puts a big pot of water over a fire and tosses in the stones. People are so curious that they each bring something to add to the pot; before long the whole village finds itself enjoying the marvelous soup together, little realizing that they were the magic that made it taste so good.

I don't have any recipes with stones in them, but I *will* give you a large collection of soup and stew recipes that make use of the best variety of fresh vegetables and other healthy plant-based ingredients. And that's some real magic.

Barley Lentil Stew

Barley Lentil Stew; A Great Lunch Or Dinner Choice

Barley is one of those grains that we don't use often enough. It is one of the oldest grains consumed by humans. Its use goes back to ancient Egypt and Africa. It was a staple in the diet of the peasants in medieval villages. Barley is high in fiber and is also an antioxidant that supports the health of your heart.

The stew also contains lentils, another ancient ingredient that is high in fiber. Combined, these items will fill you up and keep your digestive system functioning properly. This recipe produces four servings.

Ingredients:
½ onion, chopped
2 stalks celery, chopped
1 carrot, diced
1 tablespoon olive oil
3 cups vegetable stock (See recipe, Chapter 11.)
2 small red potatoes, skin on, chopped
¼ cup dry, uncooked barley
¾ cup cooked lentils

Directions:
1. Place a large pot over medium high heat and add the oil. Once it is heated, add the vegetables and sauté for three to four minutes, until slightly softened.
2. Add the vegetable stock and the potatoes and bring the pot to a boil.
3. Reduce the heat to a simmer and add the barley and lentils.
4. Simmer gently for 45 minutes, adding water if needed until the barley is plump and soft.
5. Serve hot.

Chickpea Noodle Soup

Ditalini Pasta Works Well In This Dish

This soup is a regular at my house because it is so good. It makes four servings, but I often double the recipe so I'll have leftovers to freeze for another day.

Chickpeas add fiber and protein to the soup. I use whole-wheat pasta, but you must watch it because it does not cook up as quickly as regular pasta. If you're avoiding gluten, you can also go for gluten free pasta.

Ingredients:

1 tablespoon olive or coconut oil
1 clove garlic, minced
1 onion, diced
6 stalks celery, diced
4 carrots, peeled and diced
4 cups vegetable stock (See recipe, Chapter 11.)
4 cups water
2 heaping tablespoons white miso paste
4 ounces whole-wheat pasta
1 15-ounce can chickpeas, rinsed and drained
salt and pepper to taste
2 handfuls baby spinach

Directions:

1. Place the oil in a large pot over medium high heat.

2. Sauté the garlic for one to two minutes, then add the onion and sauté for another couple minutes, until softened.
3. Add the celery and carrot and sauté for another two to three minutes.
4. Add the vegetable stock and water and bring the pot to a boil.
5. Pour in the pasta; as soon as it is cooked al dente, add the miso paste and chickpeas and turn down the heat to a simmer.
6. Season with salt and pepper to taste, simmering until everything is heated through.
7. If you are freezing your soup, stop here and let the soup cool before putting into freezer containers. However, if you plan to serve the soup immediately, toss in the spinach, turn off the heat and let the pot set there just long enough to wilt the spinach.
8. Serve the soup hot.

Creamy Carrot and White Bean Soup

This soup is so creamy like velvet. The secret is to bake the carrots first. The soup comes out a pretty pink-orange color and tastes very sweet. The white beans lend substance and more fiber, so you will feel happily full after eating a bowl. This recipe makes four servings.

Ingredients:
2 pounds carrots, peeled and chopped
2 tablespoons maple syrup
1 14-ounce can coconut milk
1½ cups vegetable stock (See recipe, Chapter 11.)
1 14-ounce can white beans (I use cannellini)
1 pinch turmeric
1 pinch curry powder
1 pinch salt
1 pinch pepper

Directions:

1. Preheat the oven to 350 degrees, Fahrenheit and line a rimmed baking sheet with parchment paper.
2. Place the chopped carrots in a bowl and pour in the maple syrup. Toss and make sure each carrot piece is coated with the syrup.
3. Spread the carrots on the baking sheet, making sure they don't overlap. Bake for 35 minutes.
4. Remove the carrots from the oven and cool for at least 15 minutes.
5. Scrape the carrots into a blender or food processor; add the coconut milk and vegetable stock and blend until smooth.
6. Add the beans, turmeric, curry, salt and pepper; blend until smooth and creamy.
7. Pour back into the pot and heat through before serving.

Creamy Leek and Potato Soup

Garnish With Kidney Beans, Cooked Parsnips and Parsley

Here's another creamy soup to add to your recipe box. Leeks have a mild onion-like flavor and look like large green onions. They are a dirty vegetable that needs to be cleaned well to keep your soup from grittiness and tasting like the earth they came from; not a pleasant texture or flavor.

To clean a leak, cut off most of the green part and also the roots at the bottom. Cut the bulb in half, lengthwise. You will see the dirt immediately. Cut the leek into small pieces and place them in a bowl of water, swishing them around to get rid of the loose dirt. Dump it into a colander and rinse again until you can see no dirt on any of the pieces. Let the leek drain and use it in the soup.

The Scots really love their leek and potato soup, but they also include chicken and change the name to cock-a-leekie soup.

Ingredients:

3 large leeks, cleaned and chopped in pieces
1 tablespoon vegan butter (or regular butter if you don't mind)
1½ tablespoons olive oil
1 pinch sea salt
1 small onion, diced
3 medium potatoes, peeled and chopped
3 cloves garlic, minced
½ teaspoon dried rosemary
1½ teaspoons dried thyme
½ teaspoon ground coriander
5 cups vegetable stock (See recipe, Chapter 11.)
1 teaspoon more sea salt
¼ teaspoon pepper
2 bay leaves
1 cup coconut milk
1 green onion, chopped

Directions:

1. Prepare the leeks and drain them well
2. Put the butter and oil in a large pot over medium heat and add a pinch of salt.
3. When the butter is melted, add the leeks and onion and sauté for five to six minutes, until soft.
4. Add the potatoes, garlic, rosemary, thyme and coriander and sauté for about three minutes.

5. Pour in the vegetable broth, salt, pepper and bay leaves and bring to a boil.
6. Immediately turn the heat down to a simmer and let it cook for 15 minutes.
7. Remove the bay leaves and pour in the coconut milk. Taste and season with salt and pepper.
8. Use an immersion blender (or process in batches in a blender) and blend until smooth and creamy.
9. Pour back into the pot if it was removed; heat through until hot.
10. Ladle into bowls and top with chopped green onion and a little more pepper.

Green Cream of Broccoli Soup

Serve With A Steamed Broccoli Floret Floating On Top

This soup is a lovely shade of green when you finish it. I usually use coconut milk because I like the flavor better than almond or soy milk. The coconut milk tends to be a little creamier and the flavor of the broccoli really comes through. This recipe makes four servings.

Ingredients:
6 cups fresh broccoli florets
1 teaspoon olive or coconut oil
1 clove garlic, chopped

1 teaspoon tamari sauce

2 cups cold coconut milk (you may need a little more if the soup is too thick)

1 teaspoon dry Italian seasoning

¼ teaspoon sea salt

¼ teaspoon ground pepper

1 dash of cayenne pepper (optional, but it does give the soup some zing)

Directions:

1. Cut up the broccoli into florets and place in a steamer basket over a pan of boiling water. Steam the florets for seven to eight minutes, until they are tender crisp.
2. Place oil in a large soup pot over medium heat and let it heat up. Add the garlic and sauté for about two minutes.
3. Add the tamari sauce and coconut milk, stir and add the steamed broccoli.
4. Add the Italian seasoning, salt and the black and cayenne pepper; turn off the heat while you use an immersion blender to process the mixture until it's smooth and creamy.
5. If the soup is too thick for your liking, add more coconut milk, two tablespoons at a time, until you get to the proper consistency.
6. Turn the burner back on over medium heat and simmer for 10 to 15 minutes.

Lemongrass Lime Mushroom Soup

Lemongrass Has A Delightfully Mild Lemon Flavor

Lemongrass is frequently used in Thai cooking, but it can be used to enhance almost any cuisine. It has a gentler lemon flavor than a regular lemon. The grass appears like a cross between a green onion and a grass reed. It is hard and tough on the outside. Those hard layers must be peeled away and discarded. Once you get down to the softer, light yellowish green part, you chop off the very bottom, using a cleaver or a very sharp knife. Peel off any more hard or ugly layers until the lemongrass is smooth.

In this recipe you use two stalks of lemongrass. One is left whole and smashed all the way up and down. Just place the stalk on a cutting board and take a large sharp knife or cleaver and lay it flat on top. Use your other hand to press down on the knife, being careful not to cut yourself. The second lemongrass stalk is thinly sliced. I would not use all the grass because that would be too much. Take the grass and cut off the hard end, then take your sharp knife and cut lengthwise up from the bottom about one to 1½ inches. It will look like you're making a fringe. Then cut across the fringe to make small minced pieces. Keep mincing until you've amassed about two tablespoons of minced lemongrass. Cut the rest of the stalk into three inch sections and freeze them for later use. This recipe makes six servings of delicious citrus-flavored mushroom soup.

162

Ingredients:
- 1 tablespoon olive oil
- 1 tablespoon sesame oil
- 2 cloves garlic, minced
- ½ red onion, finely chopped
- 1 celery stalk, finely chopped
- 1 tablespoon fresh ginger, peeled and chopped
- 1 cup shitake mushrooms, thinly sliced (do not substitute)
- 2 14-ounce cans coconut milk
- 1½ cups vegetable stock (See recipe, Chapter 11.)
- 1 small red chili pepper, seeded and minced
- 1 stalk fresh lemongrass, whole and pounded
- 1 to two tablespoons of lemongrass, minced
- Sea salt and ground pepper to taste
- 1 handful fresh basil leaves
- 1 lime, juiced
- ½ cup red bell pepper, julienned

Directions:
1. Place a soup pot over medium high heat and add the olive oil and sesame oil.
2. Sauté the garlic for one or two minutes, then add the onion, celery, ginger and mushrooms. Sauté for six minutes.
3. Add the coconut milk, vegetable broth, chili pepper, lemongrass stalk and minced lemongrass.
4. Season with salt and pepper.
5. Bring to a simmer and let it cook for around 15 minutes; you want everything to be piping hot.
6. Stir in the basil leaves and turn the heat off.
7. Squeeze in the lime juice, stir the pot and serve with a fresh basil leaf on top of each bowlful.

Meatless Irish Stew

Irish stew is normally made using lamb, but this plant-based version only uses vegetables. What makes it Irish stew, you might ask? It's the beer. Vegans can use a vegan stout, but if you aren't vegan, you can use any old stout.

This stew uses a little bit of all-purpose flour as a thickening agent. If you're avoiding flour, substitute arrowroot powder instead.

This is a hearty stew that will warm you up for long winter nights. It serves six.

Ingredients:

2 tablespoons olive oil
3 cloves garlic, chopped
1 onion, chopped
¼ cup all-purpose flour
2 to 4 cups vegetable stock (See recipe, Chapter 11.)
1 can stout beer
8 ounces mushrooms, quartered
3 carrots, peeled and chopped
2 parsnips, peeled and chopped
2½ cups baby potatoes, halved
2 bay leaves
½ cup tomato paste (See recipe, Chapter 11.)
2 teaspoons brown sugar
1 teaspoon dried thyme
½ teaspoon sea salt
¼ teaspoon ground pepper

Directions:

1. Heat a soup pot over medium heat and add the olive oil.
2. Add the garlic and sauté for about a minute.
3. Add the onion and celery and sauté for five minutes.
4. Sprinkle the flour in and stir to coat the vegetables. Cook for one minute, stirring constantly so nothing burns; you may have to turn the heat down.
5. Add two cups of stock and set the rest aside. If the soup becomes too thick, you add more stock, a bit at a time, until it reaches the desired consistency.
6. Scrape the bottom of the pot to pull up the brown bits and stir to incorporate them into the soup. Turn up the heat again, bringing the soup almost to a boil.

7. Return the heat to a simmer. Add the mushrooms, carrots, parsnips, potatoes, bay leaves and tomato paste; stir to mix.
8. Pour in the beer. It will foam up, but that's normal. Keep stirring to keep it in the pot until the foam subsides.
9. Add the brown sugar, thyme, salt and pepper; stir together.
10. Simmer for 15 to 20 minutes, until the carrots and potatoes are tender crisp. This soup is supposed to be thick, but if it is too thick, you can add more vegetable broth, two tablespoons at a time.
11. Remove the pot from the heat and remove the bay leaves, discarding them. Serve the soup hot.

Middle Eastern Eggplant and Cauliflower Stew

With Its Exotic Flavors, This Stew Will Surprise Your Taste Buds

This is an interesting stew that has some substance because of the cauliflower, but it doesn't taste overtly like cauliflower. The spices take over and give it a Middle Eastern flavor while the eggplant and chickpeas add an earthy, delicious quality. This recipe serves 4.

Ingredients:
1 teaspoon coconut or olive oil
1 onion, diced

1 eggplant, diced
2 teaspoons fresh ginger, peeled and minced
2 cloves garlic, minced
1 to 2 teaspoons fresh turmeric, minced
½ teaspoon ground cumin seed
1 teaspoon ground cinnamon
½ teaspoon ground coriander seeds
2 cups canned whole tomatoes
2 cups canned chickpeas
1 head cauliflower, chopped in bite-sized pieces
Salt and pepper to taste

Directions:

1. Place a soup pot over medium heat and add the coconut oil.
2. Once melted, sauté the onion for two to three minutes until translucent.
3. Add the eggplant and sauté for eight to 10 minutes, until the vegetables are soft.
4. Stir in the ginger, garlic and turmeric; sauté for another three minutes.
5. Add the cumin, cinnamon and coriander and stir for one more minute.
6. Crush the tomatoes with your hands and add them to the pot, along with the rinsed and drained chickpeas and the cauliflower.
7. Season with salt and pepper.
8. Simmer for 20 to 30 minutes, until the cauliflower is tender.
9. Serve the soup hot.

Old-Fashioned Comfort – Tomato Soup

My mom used to serve tomato soup with grilled cheese sandwiches on cold days when we couldn't go to school because there was too much snow. You can still give the kids this tomato soup, but for a plant-based sandwich replacement you'll want to turn back to Chapter 5.

This is definitely comfort food. At the same time, it's a healthy alternative to the high-sodium contents of the canned variety. The recipe includes white beans, as a tasty addition, but you could omit them, It makes two servings.

Ingredients:

2 tablespoons olive oil
2 cloves garlic, smashed
1 medium sized onion, chopped
1 28-ounce can of diced tomatoes (You can use fresh, just double the cooking time.)
1 15-ounce can white beans (navy or cannellini), drained and rinsed
1½ cups vegetable broth
Salt and pepper to taste

Directions:

1. Place a heavy soup pot over medium heat, pour in the olive oil and let it heat up.
2. Add the garlic and sauté for about two minutes.
3. Add the onion and sauté for three to four more minutes, until soft.
4. Stir in the tomatoes, beans and vegetable broth. Let it almost come to a boil, then reduce the heat to a simmer.
5. Simmer for 10 minutes and season with salt and pepper. Serve with a fresh basil leaf on top.

Peanut Lentil Stew

This is a version of an African stew that is made with sweet potatoes and peanuts. This plant-based version also includes lentils to "beef" it up. The recipe serves four to five people and if you like sweet potatoes, you will love this stew.

Ingredients:

1 teaspoon coconut oil
½ medium sized onion, chopped
4 cloves garlic, minced
1 inch fresh ginger, peeled and minced

2 juicy tomatoes, chopped

1 tablespoon tomato paste (See recipe, Chapter 11.)

½ teaspoon ground cumin

1 teaspoon ground coriander

⅛ teaspoon caraway seeds

⅛ teaspoon fennel seed

1 teaspoon chili powder

½ teaspoon paprika

1 teaspoon garlic powder

¼ teaspoon sea salt

¼ teaspoon ground pepper

¼ cup peanut butter (See recipe, Chapter 11.)

2 tablespoons peanuts, divided

½ cup red lentils

1 cup sweet potato, peeled and chopped

½ cup zucchini, chopped

½ cup carrots, peeled and chopped

½ cup broccoli florets

2½ cups vegetable stock (See recipe, Chapter 11.)

1 teaspoon lemon or lime juice

½ cup packed baby spinach

Directions:

1. Heat the coconut oil in a soup pot and once melted add the onion and sauté until soft.
2. Place the garlic, ginger, tomatoes, tomato paste, cumin, coriander, caraway seed, fennel seed, chili powder, paprika, garlic powder and salt and pepper in a blender or food processor and puree. Add this to the pot and cook for five to six minutes stirring frequently.
3. Add the peanut butter, half the peanuts, sweet potato, zucchini, carrot, broccoli, lentils, vegetable stock and lemon juice. Cover and simmer 10 minutes adding more water if needed.
4. Turn off the heat and add the baby spinach. Let sit two minutes and serve in bowls and garnish with the rest of the peanuts.

Plain Old Cream of Mushroom Soup

Bye-Bye Canned Soup; This Is Much Tastier

This recipe isn't plain at all because it is much tastier than the type of mushroom soup you get in a can. I like to use baby portobello mushrooms or shitake mushrooms because I like their flavor. Sometimes I combine both. If you do not wish to use the white wine in the recipe, just put three to five cups of vegetable stock in. This recipe makes four servings.

Ingredients:
    1 teaspoon coconut or olive oil
    1 clove garlic, chopped
    2 medium onions, diced
    2 pounds mushrooms, cut into bite-sized pieces
    1 cup white wine
    2 15-ounce cans coconut milk, divided
    2 to 4 cups vegetable stock (See recipe, Chapter 11.)
    5 sprigs fresh thyme (more for garnish)
    ¼ teaspoon sea salt
    ¼ teaspoon pepper

Directions:

1. Heat the oil in a soup pot over medium high heat.
2. Sauté the garlic for one to two minutes and add the onion and sauté for five more minutes
3. Add the mushrooms and sauté on medium to low for 10 to 15 minutes or until all the juice evaporates.
4. Using a slotted spoon, remove half of the mushroom, onion and garlic mixture and put in a blender.
5. Deglaze the pot with the wine scraping up all the brown bits.
6. Add one can of the coconut milk to the blender and blend the mixture until it becomes smooth.
7. Pour the blended mixture back into the soup pot.
8. Add the other can of coconut milk, two cups of the vegetable stock, thyme, salt and pepper.
9. Simmer 10 to 15 minutes. if it is too thick add more vegetable stock, two tablespoons at a time, until you reach the right consistency. Heat through and serve.

Plant-based Minestrone Soup

Minestrone is an Italian soup filled with vegetables, beans and pasta with a tomato base. I like mine chunky, so I use diced tomatoes, but if you like a smoother consistency, use pureed tomatoes. It is supposed to be rustic so the only thing I cut small is the celery so that it cooks evenly with the rest of the vegetables. A rough chop is good on everything else. This will make about six bowls. Freeze some if you have excess.

Ingredients:

4 cups gluten-free or wheat pasta (use noodles, bowties, penne or elbows)
1 tablespoons olive oil
2 cloves garlic, crushed
1 onion, chopped
2 stalks celery, thinly sliced
4 carrots, peeled and chopped
4 cups vegetable stock (See recipe, Chapter 11.)
3 cups water

1 28-ounce can diced, crushed or pureed tomatoes
1 15-ounce can cannellini beans, rinsed and drained
1 14.5 to 15-ounce can green beans, rinsed and drained
1 15-ounce can kidney beans, rinsed and drained
1 teaspoon dried oregano
1 teaspoon dried basil
2 cups fresh spinach, packed

Directions:

1. Cook the pasta per package instructions, drain and set them aside until needed.
2. Put a soup pot on the stove over medium high heat and add the oil. Sauté the garlic for about two minutes and add the onion, celery and carrots and sauté until tender crisp.
3. Add the stock, water and tomatoes and stir. Make sure nothing is sticking to the bottom of the pan.
4. Stir in the rinsed and drained beans.
5. Add the oregano and basil and once the pot starts to bubble, turn down to simmer. Keep stirring for a few minutes to be sure nothing sticks to the bottom of the pan. Simmer on low about 20 minutes.
6. Add the noodles and simmer another 10 minutes.
7. Remove from the heat and add the spinach, stirring it in and allowing it to wilt.
8. Serve the soup immediately.

Purely Vegetables Stew

The Mushrooms Give This Stew Nice Texture

This recipe makes a large batch of 12 servings, perfect for a hungry crowd. Any leftovers can be frozen for another day.

The recipe calls for red wine, but if you don't want to use wine, you can substitute vegetable stock or water. It also calls for two different types of mushrooms; I wouldn't skimp here. Each mushroom has a unique flavor and texture, which is especially helpful where there's no meat involved.

Ingredients:

    1 cup onion, diced, divided
    3 carrots, peeled and minced, divided
    3 ribs celery, minced, divided
    1 clove garlic, minced
    3¼ cups vegetable stock, divided (See recipe, Chapter 11.)
    8 ounces portobello mushrooms, sliced
    8 ounces fresh button mushrooms, sliced
    1 teaspoon Italian seasoning
    1 teaspoon dried rosemary
    ½ cup red wine
    1 15-ounce can diced tomatoes
    2 potatoes (Yukon Gold works well), peeled and chopped
    1 8-ounce can tomato sauce
    Salt and pepper to taste

1 tablespoon balsamic vinegar
1 cup frozen peas
1 tablespoon cornstarch
1 tablespoon cold water

Directions:

1. Pour a quarter cup of the vegetable stock into a large soup pot over medium heat and sauté a quarter cup of the onion, one minced carrot, one minced celery rib and the garlic until the vegetables are soft. This will take five to eight minutes.
2. Add the mushrooms and sauté until they have lost most of their liquid.
3. Stir in the Italian seasoning and the rosemary.
4. Deglaze the bottom of the pan with the wine, scraping up all the brown bits into the soup.
5. Add the remaining broth, tomatoes, potatoes, tomato sauce, the remaining carrots and celery. Turn up the heat and bring to a boil.
6. As soon as the stew begins to boil, turn it down to a simmer and add the vinegar and frozen peas. Stir to combine.
7. Place the cornstarch in a mug with the water and whisk until it is well combined. Stir this mixture into the stew while it is simmering. Continue to stir constantly until it thickens.
8. Serve while hot.

Rhubarb Stew with Lentils

Rhubarb Looks Like Red Celery But It Adds Zing To Anything

When I think of rhubarb, I usually have in mind a fruit pie or some sort of dessert. However, I've discovered that rhubarb can work quite well in savory dishes. While it has a mouth-puckering quality that my neighbor's daughter calls "sour celery", it can add a tangy sweetness to a dish. Combined with the beets in this recipe, it makes for a savory sweet and sour stew. I promise you, if you try this, you are going to like it. When guests learn what you put in the soup pot, they will be astounded. This recipe makes four servings.

Ingredients:
Steamed rice or quinoa, prepared per package instructions
1 cup dry red lentils
2 tablespoons vegetable or olive oil
4 cloves garlic, minced
1½ cups onion, diced
3 tablespoons fresh ginger, peeled and minced
1 tablespoon curry powder
2 tablespoons tamari or soy sauce (See recipe, Chapter 11.)
7 stalks rhubarb, cut into bite-sized pieces
3 cups water
2 cups vegetable stock (See recipe, Chapter 11.)
2 medium fresh beets, cut into bite-sized pieces
1 to 2 tablespoons maple syrup
½ teaspoon sea salt

¼ teaspoon ground black pepper
Cilantro for garnish

Directions:

1. Prepare the rice or quinoa and when done, set aside until needed.
2. Preheat the oven to 350 degrees, Fahrenheit.
3. Pour the lentils into a large bowl of water. Swish around until the water starts to look dirty, then drain it. Keep renewing the water and swishing it until the water no longer turns dirty. This may take up to five times. Drain the lentils well.
4. Place a soup pot over medium heat and add the oil. Let it heat up and add the garlic, sautéing for about two minutes.
5. Add the onion and ginger and sauté until the onion is translucent, about five minutes.
6. Add the curry and the tamari or soy sauce. If the mixture is too dry and begins to stick to the bottom of the pot, add three tablespoons of water.
7. Pour in the lentils, rhubarb, water and vegetable stock. Stir and bring to a boil, reducing immediately to a simmer. Let the pot simmer for 30 minutes, stirring occasionally to keep the stew from scorching.
8. While the stew is simmering, place the cut beets on a parchment-covered baking sheet and roast in the preheated oven for 20 minutes.
9. When lentils soften, add the maple syrup, salt and pepper. Toss in the beets and heat through.
10. Serve over warmed rice or quinoa.

Vegan Pho

Top Your Vegan Pho With Chopped Kale, Spinach, Or Thai Basil

Pho is a Vietnamese dish. It is normally made using beef or chicken stock, rice noodles, vegetables and thin cuts of beef or chicken, You'll find it includes a great deal of garlic as well as some lemongrass. This four-serving plant-based recipe uses vegetable stock but no meat; it's probably tastier than if it *did* have meat in it.

 This is a very filling and satisfying soup. The recipe says to char the ginger and onions under a broiler, but I don't really like them blackened. Instead, I broil them until they are dark brown but still almost raw on the inside. They taste even better if you roast them on an outdoor grill.

Ingredients:
3 inches fresh ginger, peeled and chopped
1 onion, chopped
1 10-ounce bag dehydrated shitake mushrooms
3 cups water, divided
1 tablespoon coconut oil
½ head garlic (usually about 6 to 8 cloves), each clove peeled and chopped
1 stalk lemongrass, peeled, pounded and chopped

¼ head of fennel, peeled and chopped
4 green onions, chopped
½ cup soy sauce (See recipe, Chapter 11.) or tamari sauce
4 cups vegetable broth
½ to ¾ teaspoon sea salt
8-ounces brown rice noodles, cooked per package instructions

Directions:

1. Place the ginger and onion on a nonstick-sprayed baking pan. Place in your broiler, set on high. Watch closely and remove as soon as the outsides are very brown, but the inside is still tender. This usually takes four to five minutes. Remove from the oven and set the pan aside to cool.
2. Place the mushrooms in a bowl and pour one cup of water over the top. This may not cover them, but that is fine. Let them set until you are ready for them, letting them plump up a little.
3. Pour the olive oil into a large soup pot over medium heat. Sauté the garlic, lemongrass, fennel and green onions for two to three minutes.
4. Add the soy sauce, the rest of the water, the vegetable stock and the salt.
5. Scoop out the mushrooms from the bowl and chop them slightly. Place them into the soup pot, along with the water they soaked in and bring the liquid to a slight boil.
6. Reduce the heat to a simmer and add the brown rice noodles. Simmer for five to 10 minutes, until everything is heated through.
7. Serve, topped with bean sprouts, blanched bok choy or cabbage, fresh cilantro or basil and possibly more green onions, as you wish.

Veggie Chili

Beans Provide Meaty Texture; I Top Mine With Vegan Cheddar

You can make this chili hot or not, as you like it, by adjusting the amount of chili powder and by using either jalapenos or green chilies. This chili calls for three cans of beans. You can use all three of one kind or go for some gusto and include three different kinds of bean. I tend to use kidney beans, pinto or cannellini beans and black beans.

This is one of those dishes that tastes better the longer you let it simmer. Feel free to let the spices blend in the pot, simmering longer than the required 10 minutes. The recipe makes six servings.

Ingredients:
   3 15-ounce cans beans, rinsed and drained
   1 4.5-ounce can diced green chilies or three to four jalapeno peppers, seeded and diced
   1 medium onion, diced
   1 8-ounce can tomato sauce
   1 28-ounce can diced tomatoes
   1 teaspoon garlic powder
   1 teaspoon cumin
   1 to 2 tablespoons chili powder

1 teaspoon paprika
½ teaspoon sea salt
½ teaspoon pepper

Directions:
1. Place the rinsed and drained beans in a large soup pot, along with the green chilies or jalapenos, tomato sauce and diced tomatoes.
2. Bring to a simmer and cook, stirring frequently, until the peppers are cooked through.
3. Add the garlic powder, cumin, chili powder, paprika, salt and pepper; stir to combine.
4. Simmer for at least another 10 minutes before serving while hot.

White Bean-Kale-Lemon Stew

This stew is light and refreshing. That may sound unusual for a stew, but it comes from the lightness of the white beans and kale and the brightness of the lemon. Feel free to substitute baby leaf lettuce for the kale if you desire. This recipe makes four servings.

Ingredients:
1 tablespoon olive oil
4 cloves garlic, minced
1 medium onion, finely chopped
1½ teaspoons dried rosemary
2 tablespoons arrowroot powder or cornstarch
4 cups vegetables broth
2 15-ounce cans white beans, rinsed and drained
½ teaspoon sea salt
½ teaspoon pepper
1 bunch kale, stalks removed and chopped (about 6 large leaves)
1 medium lemon

Directions:
1. Heat the olive oil in a large soup pot over medium heat. Add the garlic and sauté for two minutes.

2. Add the onion and sauté for three to five minutes, until translucent.
3. Add the rosemary and arrowroot powder and coat the vegetables.
4. Slowly pour the broth into the pot, stirring constantly so that lumps do not form.
5. Add the beans, salt and pepper and keep stirring while the mixture thickens.
6. Once thickened, add the kale. Cut the lemon in half and squeeze both halves into the soup. Then, throw in the rinds and simmer for 10 minutes.
7. Remove the lemon rinds before serving.

The next chapter presents some wonderful meatless main dishes that you can enjoy with your friends and family.

Chapter 8: Main Dishes That Everyone Loves

Although you can probably use almost every recipe in this book as a main dish, The recipes in this chapter tend to mirror meat-based dishes, but without the meat. You'll find dishes reminiscent of meatloaf, crab cakes, curry and even chicken nuggets. You'll enjoy cauliflower steaks and flavors like teriyaki, sweet and sour, burgundy, barbecue and curry. You really won't miss the meat in these dishes.

Asian-Inspired Teriyaki Veggie Burgers with Shitake Mushrooms

This tasty plant-based burger is one of my favorites. It has flavor to spare. If you don't want to use English muffins, you can also wrap it in a tortilla. The spices make this burger special and the texture is almost like hamburger. This recipe makes four servings.

Ingredients:
1 small sweet potato, about ½ pound
¾ cup old-fashioned rolled oats
1 15-ounce can kidney beans, rinsed and drained
2 green onions, thinly sliced
½ cup shelled sunflower seeds
½ teaspoon kosher salt
½ teaspoon garlic powder
2 teaspoons paprika
1¾ tablespoons mirin, divided
2 tablespoons soy sauce, divided (See recipe, Chapter 11.)
4 shiitake mushrooms, stems removed
1 tablespoon olive or coconut oil
2 teaspoons sriracha
¼ cup vegan mayonnaise (See recipe, Chapter 11.)
Whole wheat English muffins
Alfalfa sprouts

Directions:

1. Preheat the oven to 375 degrees, Fahrenheit.
2. Prick the sweet potato with a fork and heat on high in the microwave for about eight minutes. Turn the potato over and microwave it for eight more minutes or until cooked through. Cool and cut in half lengthwise.
3. Spread out the oats on a cutting board and chop them coarsely. Pour into a mixing bowl.
4. Rinse and drain the beans and place them in the bowl with the oats.
5. Chop the green onions and add them to the bowl.
6. Add the sunflower seeds, salt, garlic powder, paprika, 1½ tablespoons of the mirin and 1½ tablespoons of the soy sauce; mix everything together with your hands, mashing the beans.
7. Remove the skin from the cooked sweet potato and put it in the bowl as well. Mix everything together with your hands.
8. Shape four patties and set them on a rimmed baking sheet that has been covered with parchment paper. Bake for 15 minutes on one side, turn and cook for another 15 minutes on the other side. Cool for five minutes.
9. While the patties are cooking, slice the four mushroom caps and use the stems to make vegetable broth.
10. Set a skillet over medium heat, place in it the oil and let it warm up.
11. Add the remaining mirin and soy sauce to the skillet, then add the mushrooms and sauté for about a minute.
12. In a bowl, mix the sriracha with the mayonnaise.
13. Place the burgers on an English muffin with mushroom mixture on top and alfalfa sprouts on top of that. Put some of the sriracha mixture on the inside of the muffin top and use it to close the sandwich.

Barbeque Bean Tacos with Tropical Salsa

This is a lovely tropical recipe that uses tortillas. You'll fill them with sweetened pinto beans and delicious pineapple, making a tropical salsa you can also use with other dishes. This recipe yields four tropical tacos.

Ingredients:
2 15-ounce cans pinto beans (substitution: white beans)
1 tablespoon maple syrup
2 tablespoons prepared Dijon mustard
¾ cup ketchup (See recipe, Chapter 11.)
½ teaspoon chili powder
½ teaspoon garlic powder
¾ teaspoon sea salt, divided
1 20-ounce can pineapple chunks, packed in juice
¼ cup cilantro, finely chopped (plus more for garnish)
¼ cup red onion, minced
3 radishes, stemmed and thinly sliced
1 small green cabbage, cored and thinly sliced
1 lime, cut into wedges
4 corn tortillas

Directions:
1. Drain and rinse the beans and pour into a heavy skillet.

2. Add the maple syrup, mustard, ketchup, chili powder, garlic powder and a half teaspoon of salt. Heat on low, stirring frequently, until the mixture heats through and thickens.
3. Meanwhile, drain and chop the pineapple chunks and put them in a bowl.
4. Add the cilantro, onion and the remaining salt and stir together.
5. Take a tortilla and place a fourth of the bean mixture on the side. Sprinkle with the radish and cabbage mixture and top with the pineapple mixture. Garnish the tops with more cilantro. Serve with lime wedges.

Burgundy Mushroom Sauce Over Polenta

This dish reminds me of beef burgundy without the beef. Different vegetables, including mushrooms, are used instead. Serve it over polenta (see Chapter 11), brown rice, or quinoa. This recipe makes four savory and delicious servings.

Ingredients:
1 tablespoon olive oil
1 medium red onion, chopped
4 cloves garlic, minced
2 large carrots, peeled, cut in half and thinly sliced
24 ounces (3 8-ounce packages) Cremini mushrooms, sliced
1 teaspoon dry mustard
½ teaspoon dried rosemary
½ teaspoon dried thyme
½ teaspoon sea salt
½ teaspoon ground black pepper
1½ cups red wine
1 15-ounce can diced tomatoes
2 tablespoon Worcestershire sauce (See recipe, Chapter 11.)
4 green onions, chopped
1 cup unsweetened non-dairy milk or vegetable broth
¼ cup parsley, chopped

Directions:

1. In a large pot over medium heat, heat the olive oil and the onion. Sauté for two to three minutes.
2. Add the garlic, carrots, dry mustard, rosemary, thyme, salt and pepper and sauté until the mushrooms turn golden and lose most of their liquid.
3. Deglaze with the wine; scrape the brown bits up from the bottom of the pan.
4. Add the tomatoes, Worcestershire sauce and green onions. Cook to reduce the liquid by half.
5. Make some polenta, rice, or quinoa and set it aside until ready to serve.
6. If you're using polenta, stir in enough of the non-dairy milk or vegetable broth until it becomes the consistency of mashed potatoes.
7. To serve, spoon the mushroom sauce over the polenta and sprinkle with the parsley.

Carrot Brown Rice Casserole With Spinach

The Antioxidants In Carrots May Reduce Your Risk Of Cancer

I enjoy taking casseroles to pot luck dinners and this one is always a big hit. It is sweet and savory at the same time and tastes a little like peanuts. The sweetness comes from the carrots.

Ingredients:
1 bunch fresh spinach leaves, chopped
2 tablespoons vegetable stock (See recipe, Chapter 11.)
3 cups shredded carrots
1 large onion, chopped
1 teaspoon sea salt

½ teaspoon dry thyme

1½ teaspoons garlic powder

¼ cup smooth peanut butter (See recipe, Chapter 11.)

3 cups water or vegetable stock

3 cups cooked brown rice

1 tablespoon soy sauce (See recipe, Chapter 11.)

¾ cup whole-grain crumbs

Directions:

1. Coat the inside of a two-quart casserole with nonstick spray and preheat the oven to 350 degrees, Fahrenheit.
2. Spread the spinach on the bottom of the casserole dish.
3. Heat a large pot over medium high heat and add the two tablespoons of vegetable broth. This will keep everything from sticking to the pan.
4. Add the onions and carrots and sauté for five minutes.
5. Add the salt, thyme and garlic powder and stir in.
6. Add the peanut butter and water or vegetable stock and whisk until smooth.
7. Stir in the soy sauce along with the breadcrumbs and stir well.
8. Pour this on top of the spinach and cover with a lid or foil.
9. Bake for 45 minutes and take out of the oven. Let cool for 10 minutes, remove the cover and serve.

Cashew Topped Vegetable Stuffed Peppers

Serve Stuffed Peppers With Or Without The Tomato Sauce

I love stuffed peppers and these are filled with flavorful kidney beans, sun-dried tomatoes, Swiss chard and more, all swimming in a delightful tomato sauce. Red peppers are used and chopped in half lengthwise to provide a solid bottom. This recipe makes six servings.

Ingredients:
1 tablespoon olive oil
2 cloves garlic, chopped
1 medium onion, chopped
8 ounces mushrooms, sliced
2 to three large Swiss chard leaves, coarsely chopped
1 15-ounce can kidney beans, rinsed and drained
8 sun-dried tomatoes, soaked in hot water until reconstituted and chopped
1 to 2 cups tomato sauce
1½ cups cooked brown rice or quinoa
3 large red peppers, cut into half lengthwise
⅓ cup raw cashews, finely chopped

Directions:
1. Preheat the oven to 375 degrees, Fahrenheit.
2. Place the olive oil in a heated skillet and add the garlic, sautéing for two minutes.
3. Add the onions and mushrooms and sauté until the onion is soft.
4. Add the chard and beans and cook until the chard wilts.
5. Add the drained and chopped sun-dried tomatoes, tomato sauce and cooked rice or quinoa. Stir to combine everything.
6. Fill the pepper cups with the mixture and place in a baking dish that has been sprayed with nonstick spray. Cover with foil.
7. Bake for 40 minutes, remove from the oven and sprinkle cashews over the top. Bake for another 10 minutes.
8. Cool for 10 minutes before serving.

Coconut Curry With Cauliflower and Tomato

This Curry Will Put Spice Into Your Life

This is an Indian curry dish that uses sweet potatoes, cauliflower, chickpeas and plum tomatoes. It's spicy, as curry should be. I use full-fat coconut milk in this dish because it requires the richness. This recipe serves four to six people.

Ingredients:

Cooked brown rice for serving
2 tablespoons olive oil
1 onion, chopped
1 pound (about 4 cups) sweet potato, unpeeled but chopped
1 head cauliflower (about 4 cups), chopped
1 teaspoon kosher salt, divided
1 tablespoon garam masala
1 teaspoon cumin
¼ teaspoon cayenne pepper
2 tablespoons curry powder
1 23-ounce jar diced San Marzano plum tomatoes
1 15-ounce can full-fat coconut milk
1 15-ounce can chickpeas, rinsed and drained
4 cups fresh spinach leaves
Cilantro for garnish

Directions:
1. Heat the oil in a large pot over medium heat.
2. Sauté the onions for about three minutes, then add the sweet potato and sauté for another 3 minutes.
3. Add the cauliflower and a half teaspoon of the salt; sauté for five minutes.
4. Add the garam marsala, cumin, cayenne pepper and curry powder; stir to mix thoroughly.
5. Pour in the plum tomatoes, including their juice and the coconut milk; bring to a boil.
6. Reduce the heat and simmer, covered, for about 10 minutes. The cauliflower should be soft.
7. Add the chickpeas and spinach leaves, along with the rest of the salt; stir until the spinach wilts and the chickpeas are heated through.
8. Serve over brown rice and garnish with cilantro.

Greek Style Stuffed Sweet Potatoes

This recipe makes eight halves of a sweet potato, with two halves per person, for a total of four servings. You'll bake the sweet potatoes and make a Greek-inspired salad topping with olives, tomatoes, onions and cucumber, along with mint and drizzling the whole thing with a Tahini dressing.

Ingredients:
4 sweet potatoes
½ red onion, chopped
1 cucumber, peeled and chopped
2 large tomatoes, chopped
1 small jar Kalamata olives, chopped
3 tablespoons fresh mint, chopped
1 lime, juiced
1 clove garlic, processed into a paste
2 tablespoons lemon juice
⅓ cup Tahini sauce
¼ teaspoon salt
2 to 6 tablespoons lukewarm water
1 15-ounce can chickpeas, drained and rinsed

Directions:
1. Preheat the oven to 375 degrees, Fahrenheit.
2. Cut the cleaned sweet potatoes in half lengthwise and place them, with cut side down, on a greased baking sheet. Bake for 20 to 30 minutes, until tender when poked with a fork. Remove from the oven to cool.
3. In a bowl, combine the onions, cucumber, tomatoes, olives, mint and lime juice. Mix well and set the bowl aside.
4. In another bowl, combine the garlic, lemon juice, Tahini sauce and salt. Start adding the water with two tablespoons and see if it becomes the right consistency. If it is thick and pasty, add more of the water up to six tablespoons. Set the mixture aside.
5. To assemble, place two potato halves on a plate right side up and mash with a fork lightly. Place the onion, cucumber tomato and olive mixture on top. Sprinkle with chickpeas and end up with the Tahini mixture on top and serve.

Imitation Crab Cakes With Tofu

They Look And Taste Like Crab Cakes But Are Made From Tofu

These fake crab cakes are made with no crab at all. They contain tofu seasoned with herbs and vegetables; that's what makes them taste like crab. This recipe yields six servings.

Ingredients:
2 tablespoons ground flaxseed
4 tablespoons water
1 block tofu
½ cup red bell pepper, diced
½ cup yellow bell pepper, diced
¾ cup red onion, diced
1½ cups celery diced
¼ cup flat leaf parsley, chopped
1 tablespoons capers, drained
½ teaspoon Worcestershire sauce ((See recipe, Chapter 11.)
¼ teaspoon hot sauce (See recipe, Chapter 11.)
1½ teaspoons Old Bay seasoning
¼ cup vegetable stock (See recipe, Chapter 11.)
salt and pepper to taste
1 tablespoon lemon juice
½ tablespoon lemon zest
½ cup dry wheat bread crumbs
2 tablespoons Dijon mustard
Mango salsa, for accompaniment

Directions:
1. Combine the flaxseed and water and let it soak until ready to use.
2. Cut the tofu block in half lengthwise, pressing each half between paper towels and wrapping in newspaper to make it as dry as possible. Place something heavy on top and let it rest for 20 minutes.
3. Put the red and yellow bell pepper, the onion, celery, parsley, capers, Worcestershire sauce, hot sauce, Old Bay seasoning, vegetable stock, salt and pepper in a large pot over medium low heat. Cook for 15 minutes or until everything is soft. Cool to room temperature.
4. Place the tofu in a large bowl and mash it into small pieces

5. Add the lemon juice, lemon zest, breadcrumbs, mustard and the flaxseed, including the water. Mix well.
6. Add the vegetable mixture and mix well.
7. Cover the bowl and let it rest in the refrigerator for 30 minutes.
8. Preheat the oven to 375 degrees, Fahrenheit and cover a baking sheet with parchment paper.
9. Remove the mixture from the refrigerator and shape it into balls, place them on the parchment paper and press down to flatten.
10. Bake for five minutes on each side and serve with mango salsa.

Lentil and Mushroom Loaf (Fake Meatloaf)

Lentil Meatloaf Looks Meaty But Has No Meat And Tastes Divine

This "meatloaf" recipe has the texture of a meatloaf made with ground beef, but the flavor is even better than that. It is not greasy, but light and very flavorful. It contains both red and green lentils; this is essential for gaining the correct texture. Measure the lentils after they are cooked. Use portobello, cremini, white or button mushrooms and measure these after they are chopped. The mixture should just hold together in a loaf shape as if it were made with ground beef. Do not use too much water or it will become a soggy mess. This recipe makes eight thick slices of loaf. Servings eight thick slices

Ingredients:

2 cloves garlic, finely chopped

1 small onion, chopped

3 cups mushrooms, finely chopped

1 cup green lentils, already cooked

1 cup red lentils, already cooked

½ cup old-fashioned rolled oats

¼ cup ground flaxseed

1 tablespoon Tamari or soy sauce (See recipe, Chapter 11.)

2 tablespoons dried thyme

½ teaspoon salt

¼ teaspoon pepper

2 tablespoons to ½ cup water

Directions:

1. Preheat the oven to 370 degrees, Fahrenheit.
2. Place the garlic, onion and mushrooms in a large mixing bowl.
3. Add the green and red lentils, oats, flaxseed, Tamari, thyme, salt and pepper; mix well with your hands. The mixture may be a little crumbly.
4. Add water, a little bit at a time and up to a half cup as needed until the mixture starts to stick together like a regular meatloaf. Add two tablespoons first, then add by two-tablespoon increments until the loaf gains the proper texture.
5. Place a strip of parchment paper on the bottom of the pan that extends up both sides and out of the pan on the small sides. This creates a sling that you can grasp to pull out the loaf after it's cooked.
6. Pack the loaf mixture into the pan and bake for 50 to 60 minutes.
7. Remove from oven and cool for 15 minutes. Lift the loaf out of the pan and set it on a cutting board to slice Serve while warm.

Meatless Chick Nuggets

These Nuggets Are Made With Chickpeas Instead Of Chicken

Kids of all ages enjoy chicken nuggets. Thanks to creative cookery, you can now make nuggets without any chicken at all. The magic is worked with breadcrumbs and chickpeas. Yes, I've at least managed to include some "chick" in the ingredients and still keep it meatless!

These nuggets taste delicious by themselves, but you can dip them any number of plant-based sauces found in Chapter 11, to make them even better.

This recipe calls for whole-wheat bread crumbs, which are easily made by leaving a piece of bread out overnight to dry and pulsing it in the food processor or blender. While you can substitute panko breadcrumbs for the crumbs in the filling, our taste testers reported that the whole-wheat crumbs made for a moister inner nugget.

You'll also want to use panko bread crumbs as listed in the ingredients. I do not substitute these with anything else, because the panko makes the nuggets crispy, just like what you get in a fast food restaurant. I have sometimes been able to use whole-wheat panko crumbs; they work just as well. The recipe makes 20 pieces.

Ingredients:
1 15.5-ounce can chickpeas, rinsed and drained
½ teaspoon garlic powder
1 teaspoon granulated onion
1 tablespoon nutritional yeast
1 tablespoon whole-wheat bread crumbs (optional: substitute panko bread crumbs)
½ cup panko bread crumbs

Directions:
1. Preheat the oven to 350 degrees, Fahrenheit and cover a rimmed baking pan with parchment paper.
2. Place the drained chickpeas in a food processor and pulse four to five times.
3. Add the garlic powder, granulated onion, nutritional yeast and the tablespoon of whole-wheat bread crumbs to the processor and process until you get a chunky, grainy mixture that sticks together.
4. Scoop out by teaspoonfuls and form balls.
5. Roll the balls in the panko crumbs and set on the baking sheet, flattening each ball so it looks more like a chicken nugget. Be sure to space them apart so they do not touch each other.
6. Bake for 20 minutes, remove from the oven and flip each nugget over with tongs. Return to the oven for 10 more minutes.
7. Cool for a few minutes and then serve with honey, barbecue sauce or Ranch dipping sauce.

Portobello Bolognese With Zucchini Noodles

Zucchini Noodles Lack The Carbohydrates of Regular Noodles

Mushrooms are the star of this bolognaise sauce, with a supporting actor of zucchini noodles. You can use the sauce over regular wheat noodles if you like, but zucchini noodles are even more delicious and they're easy to make. They do have a different texture than regular pasta.

If you don't have a spiralizer, you can take the skin off the zucchini and then use a sharp knife to cut thin ribbons. Drop the zucchini ribbons into cold water for a few minutes. Then, drain them and toss the ribbons into the skillet as directed. This recipe makes four delicious servings.

Ingredients:

    3 tablespoons olive oil, divided
    ½ cup onion, minced
    3 cloves of garlic, minced
    ½ cup carrot, peeled and minced
    ½ cup celery, minced
    6 portobello mushroom caps, stems removed and finely chopped
    ½ teaspoon Kosher salt
    ½ teaspoon ground pepper
    1 tablespoon tomato paste (See recipe, Chapter 11.)
    1 28-ounce can crushed plum tomatoes

¼ teaspoon red pepper flakes, crushed (optional)
½ cup fresh basil leaves, finely chopped with more left whole for garnish
2 teaspoons dried oregano
4 medium zucchini

Directions:

1. Heat two tablespoons of the olive oil in a large skillet over medium high heat.
2. Add the onion, garlic, carrot and celery; sauté for about five minutes or until the onion turns translucent.
3. Add the mushrooms and sauté for another six to seven minutes, until the mushrooms shrink and lose their liquid. Stir constantly so they don't burn but turn a golden hue.
4. Stir in the tomato paste and cook, stirring frequently, for about two minutes.
5. Pour in the crushed tomatoes, red pepper flakes, basil and oregano. Reduce the heat to a simmer, cooking very low until the sauce thickens.
6. While the pot simmers, create the zucchini noodles and put them in cold water until they're all made. Drain the noodles and use tongs to place them in a skillet with a little water at the bottom. Toss and add some salt and pepper. They will only take a few minutes to soften and warm over medium heat.
7. Divide the noodles among four bowls and serve with the sauce on top; add a basil leaf on top as garnish.

Pot Roast Made with Portobello Mushrooms

Portobello Mushrooms Can Replace Meat In Some Recipes

Portobello mushrooms are very meaty making them a versatile vegetable to use like meat. This dish makes you think the portobellos are actually pot roast. It includes everything you would want with pot roast including the potatoes and carrots and tastes divine. It makes four servings.

Ingredients:
½ cup red wine, divided
4 large portobello mushroom caps, sliced into ¾-inch pieces
2 cloves garlic, smashed
1 large onion, sliced
1 teaspoon dried basil
1 teaspoon rubbed sage
3 tablespoons flour (I use white flour, but you can substitute whole grain flour)
3 cups vegetable stock, divided (See recipe, Chapter 11.)
½ teaspoon sea salt
½ teaspoon ground black pepper
4 large carrots, peeled and cut into thick pieces
4 large potatoes, peeled and cut into bite-sized pieces
2 teaspoons Worcestershire sauce (See recipe, Chapter 11.)
1 sprig fresh rosemary
4 sprigs fresh thyme

Directions:

1. Preheat the oven to 350 degrees, Fahrenheit.
2. In a large saucepan, heat a quarter cup of wine with the portobello slices and let them cook down and brown, stirring frequently. Pour into a bowl and set aside.
3. Deglaze the pan the mushrooms were in, using the remaining red wine; add the garlic and onions. Sauté until the onions wilt and start to brown. Transfer to a different bowl and set it aside.
4. In a small bowl, whisk together the basil, sage and flour. Whisk in a quarter cup of the vegetable stock to make a sloppy paste and scrape all of it into the same saucepan you used for the mushrooms.
5. Stir constantly over medium heat and gradually add the remaining stock to create a gravy. Keep whisking to prevent lumps.
6. When the gravy starts to boil, turn off the heat and add the salt and pepper. If it seems too dry add a little extra stock and stir to combine.
7. Pour the mushroom mixture into the gravy and then add the onion mixture. Stir well.
8. Add the carrots, potatoes and Worcestershire sauce, stirring to combine.
9. Pour into a 2-quart glass casserole coated with nonstick spray. Top with the rosemary and thyme sprigs and cover with a lid or with foil.
10. Bake for one hour, then serve.

Quesadilla With Black Beans and Sweet Potato

This simple yet pleasantly delicious main dish is made out of a sweet potato and some black beans. It yields two servings, but can be easily multiplied to make more. And you'll want more, once you've tasted it.

Ingredients:

1 medium-sized sweet potato, peeled and cut into cubes

3 teaspoons taco seasoning

4 whole-wheat tortillas

½ of a 15-ounce can of black beans, drained and rinsed
Salsa for serving (see Chapter 11 for the recipe)

Directions:
1. Bring a large pot of water to boil and drop in the sweet potato.
2. Boil for 10 to 20 minutes or until soft.
3. Drain the sweet potato and put in a bowl.
4. Add the taco seasoning and mash well.
5. To assemble the quesadilla, spread the sweet potato mixture on the tortilla.
6. Add the black beans and press them onto the potato mixture.
7. Cover with another tortilla.
8. Heat a nonstick skillet over medium high heat and lay the tortilla in it. Toast on both sides and serve immediately.

Quinoa-stuffed Acorn Squash

Stuffed Acorn Squash Is a Fall Favorite

Acorn squash has a lovely taste and adding exotic spices like cinnamon and cardamom only enhances that flavor. This is a main dish sweetened with raisins and made crunchy with nuts. It'll bring back memories of autumns past. The recipe makes four servings.

Ingredients:

½ cup quinoa, cooked per package instructions
2 acorn squash
⅛ cup water
1 large onion, chopped
⅛ teaspoon ground cloves
⅛ teaspoon ground cardamom
½ teaspoon ground ginger
1 teaspoon ground cinnamon
½ cup raisins
⅓ cup walnuts or pecans, chopped
½ teaspoon sea salt
¼ teaspoon ground black pepper

Directions:

1. Preheat the oven to 350 degrees, Fahrenheit and pre-cook the quinoa. Set it aside until ready to use.
2. Poke the squash with a fork or knife to let the steam out (and to avoid a squash explosion). Place on a microwave safe dish and microwave on high for three to four minutes. This will soften the squash before you cut into it.
3. Let the squash cool for five minutes and then cut it in half. Carefully remove the seeds as they will still be hot. Place the halves, cut side down, on a parchment-lined baking sheet. Bake for 30 to 40 minutes, until the squash is soft.
4. While squash is cooking, pour the water into a skillet over medium high heat and sauté the onion.
5. Reduce the heat to low and add the cloves, cardamom, ginger and cinnamon, stirring to mix. Turn off the heat and set the mixture aside until the squash is finished baking.
6. Once the squash is soft inside, remove it from the oven, but do not turn off the heat. As soon as it can be handled, carefully scoop the squash meat from the shell without damaging the skin. Mash the squash meat.
7. Add the squash meat to the onion spice mix in the skillet and turn the heat back on to medium high, stirring to mix.

8. Add the raisins and nuts and stir while heating through. Season with salt and pepper.
9. Turn off the heat and pack the shells with the mixture in the pan. Put the squash shells back on the baking sheet, cover everything with foil and bake for another 20 minutes before serving.

Spicy Corn and Spinach Casserole

Anyone who likes Southwestern style corn dishes will enjoy this casserole. It is mildly spicy and fully satisfying. The recipe serves five to six people.

Ingredients:
1½ cups water
¾ cup unsweetened soy milk, divided
1¼ cups cornmeal
1 14-ounce block tofu, drained and rinsed
3 cloves garlic, minced
1 10-ounce package frozen corn, thawed, divided
2 4.5-ounce cans mild chilies, diced
1 10-ounce package frozen spinach, thawed, with the liquid squeezed out
1 teaspoon baking powder
½ teaspoon cayenne pepper
½ teaspoon cumin
½ teaspoon salt
½ teaspoon pepper
Salsa as accompaniment (See recipe, Chapter 11.)

Directions:
1. Preheat the oven to 450 degrees, Fahrenheit.
2. Heat the water and a half cup of the soy milk in a medium saucepan, bringing it almost to a boil. Turn off the burner and slowly whisk in the cornmeal, letting It thicken. Scrape out into a bowl and set it aside until ready to use.
3. Wrap the tofu in a paper towel and press down to extract most of the liquid. This may require repeating several times, with fresh paper towels.

202

4. When the tofu is as dry as you can get it, place it in a food processor, along with the garlic, one cup of corn and the remaining soy milk. Process until smooth, then pour it into the bowl with the cornmeal, folding it in to combine thoroughly.
5. To the same bowl, add the rest of the corn, the chilies, spinach, baking powder, cayenne pepper, cumin, salt and pepper. The mixture will be thick but needs to be combined well. Use your muscles.
6. Pour the mixture into an oiled baking dish and bake for 60 to 70 minutes. The edges should be crispy and the middle should jiggle just a little bit.
7. Let the casserole stand for 20 minutes before serving with salsa.

Steaks of Cauliflower With Pea Puree

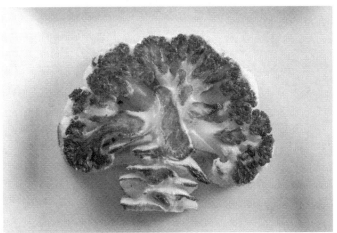

Roasted Cauliflower Steaks Are Delicious With Sauce

This is a unique dish that will have everyone wanting more. The cauliflower is sliced into flat steaks so all the lovely swirls of the vegetable can be easily seen. My nephew commented that it looks like brains, which makes it a fun entrée to serve on Halloween. However, you'll enjoy eating it any time of year.

The cauliflower steaks are topped with a delicate pea puree that is fresh and tasty. This recipe is only supposed to serve two people, but if you present it with a side dish or a salad, it can feed as many as four.

Ingredients:
2 heads cauliflower
5 teaspoons olive oil, divided
½ teaspoon coriander
1 teaspoon paprika
¼ teaspoon black pepper
1 small onion, chopped
1 10-ounce bag frozen green peas
¼ cup unsweetened soy or almond milk
2 tablespoons fresh parsley, chopped

Directions:
1. Preheat the oven to 425 degrees, Fahrenheit and line baking sheets with parchment paper.
2. Remove the bottom core from the cauliflower. Stand a head upright on its base and cut it in half down the middle. Slice steaks from each side, about ¾-inch thick.
3. Lay the steaks flat on a baking sheet and repeat the process with the second head of cauliflower.
4. Brush two teaspoons of olive oil onto the steaks and sprinkle with the coriander, paprika and pepper. Flip the steaks do the same with the other side.
5. Bake for 15 minutes, then remove from the oven and flip the steaks over. Return them to the oven and bake for 15 more minutes.
6. While the steaks are baking, prepare the pea puree by placing a teaspoon of olive oil in a skillet over medium heat. Sauté the onion until it is translucent but do not let it brown.
7. Microwave the peas until they are plump and hot.
8. Place the onion, peas, soy milk and parsley in a blender and process until smooth.
9. Serve the puree, poured over the cauliflower steaks.

Sweet and Spicy Mushroom Quinoa Pilaf

A dressing including vinegar, maple syrup, lemon juice and Dijon mustard is what makes this dish. You can substitute rice vinegar or step it up with champagne vinegar, instead. The almonds lend a little crunch and the peas and sun-dried tomatoes give it fresh color and flavor. This dish serves six.

Ingredients:

2¼ cups vegetable stock, divided (See recipe, Chapter 11.)
8-ounces mushrooms, cleaned and sliced
1 cup quinoa (uncooked)
1 cup frozen green peas
¾ cup sun-dried tomatoes, soaked in hot water for 30 minutes, drained and sliced
⅓ cup slivered almonds
¼ cup rice vinegar
1 teaspoon maple syrup
½ of a lemon, juiced
1 teaspoon Dijon mustard
¼ teaspoon salt
¼ teaspoon pepper

Directions:

1. Put a quarter cup of the vegetable stock in a large skillet over medium heat and sauté the mushrooms until they are cooked through and have shrunken slightly.
2. Add the uncooked quinoa and the remaining vegetable stock and bring to a boil. Reduce to a simmer and cook for 15 minutes or until the stock is completely absorbed and the quinoa plumps up.
3. Add the peas, sun-dried tomatoes and almonds; stir until heated through. Remove from the heat.
4. In a large bowl, whisk together the vinegar, maple syrup, lemon juice, salt and pepper.
5. Pour this dressing over the quinoa mixture and toss to coat. Serve and listen to the oohs and aahs of your guests.

Thai Tofu With Peanut Butter Sauce

Tofu Takes On The Flavor Of Its Sauce

Tofu takes on the flavor of what you put into a dish and gives it some bulk and nutritional elements. Make sure to use firm tofu in this dish that doesn't break apart easily. It lends the dish a nice texture, while the sauce imparts a pleasant peanutty flavor. The dish serves five to six people.

Ingredients:

14-ounces firm tofu
1½ tablespoons olive oil
3½ teaspoons maple syrup
¼ cup rice vinegar
1 tablespoon soy sauce (See recipe, Chapter 11) or tamari
¼ cup warm water, ranging up to ½ cup
2 tablespoons fresh cilantro, finely chopped
3 cloves garlic, minced
1 teaspoon crushed red pepper flakes
½ cup plus two tablespoons creamy peanut butter (See recipe, Chapter 11.)
1½ cups fresh spinach leaves, chopped
Prepared rice or quinoa for serving

Directions:

1. Cut the block of tofu in half and place each half between a couple paper towels. Press and squeeze both halves to remove any excess liquid, but do not break the tofu.
2. Cut the tofu into half-inch cubes
3. Place the olive oil in a skillet and add the tofu. Fry over medium heat, stirring gently until the tofu turns golden brown and the liquid in the pan has evaporated. Set the tofu aside, still in its pan.
4. In a bowl, whisk together the maple syrup, rice vinegar, soy sauce or tamari, a quarter cup of the warm water, the cilantro, garlic and red pepper flakes. Add the peanut butter and whisk until well combined. If it is too thick, add the rest of the warm water gradually, until it reaches the right consistency.
5. Place the skillet with the tofu back over low heat. Add the spinach and let it wilt.
6. Pour the peanut sauce over the mixture and simmer for five to 10 minutes. IF the sauce thickens too much, add more water to thin it.
7. Serve over rice or quinoa as desired.

Walnut Matzah Loaf

Matzah Is Made From Wheat, Spelt, Barley, Rye, or Oats

You use matzah for this delicious walnut loaf or opt for whole-grain crumbs instead. Either way it is very good. It is also possible to switch the walnuts for almonds. This does require an egg

207

replacer powder found at most natural food stores. It serves four to six people.

Ingredients:
2 tablespoons vegetable stock (See recipe, Chapter 11.)
1 medium onion, finely chopped
1½ cups matzah meal or whole-grain breadcrumbs
1 cup ground walnuts
2 tablespoons fresh parsley, chopped
1 tablespoon egg replacer (powder)
1 tablespoon ground flaxseed
1 teaspoon salt
2 tablespoons tomato paste (See recipe, Chapter 11.)
1½ cups unsweetened soy milk or other plant milk (I prefer almond milk)

Directions:
1. Line a standard loaf pan with parchment paper, extending it up the long sides of the pan in order to create handles you can use to lift the baked loaf out of the pan.
2. Heat the vegetable stock in a large skillet over medium heat. Add the onion and sauté until translucent.
3. In a bowl, combine the matzah or breadcrumbs, walnuts, parsley, egg replacer powder, flaxseed, salt and tomato paste; mix well.
4. Pour in the milk and sautéed onions and combine well. use your hands to mix everything together, then pack the mixture into the loaf pan.
5. Preheat the oven to 350 degrees, Fahrenheit and let the pan set for 30 minutes before placing it in the oven.
6. Bake for one hour, then remove the pan from the oven and let it set for 10 to 15 minutes.
7. Extract the loaf from the pan using the parchment handles, slice and serve.

Chapter 9: Delicious Snacks and Incredible Appetizers

Plant-based snacks are as good for you as they are delicious. This chapter contains a bunch of great snacks that can double as appetizers for parties. I've included dips, chips, bites, mini pizzas and even a popcorn snack made out of cauliflower. You won't down any of these goodies, they're that good.

Black Bean Dip

Sprinkle Fresh Cilantro On Top Of Your Bean Dip

This spicy dip makes enough for 10 servings and it looks just as pretty as it is delicious. The recipe calls for Ro-tel, which is a brand of tomatoes with chilies in it. If you cannot find Ro-tel, just use a can of tomatoes and mix in a small can of green chilies. Most grocery stores do carry it and it is often found in with other canned tomatoes or with the Mexican foods.

Ingredients:
2 15-ounce cans black beans, rinsed and drained

1 jalapeno pepper, seeded and minced
½ of a red bell pepper, seeded and diced
½ of a yellow bell pepper, seeded and diced
½ of s small red onion, diced
1 cup fresh cilantro, finely chopped
Zest of 1 lime
Juice of 1 lime
1 10-ounce can Ro*tel, drained
½ teaspoon Kosher salt
¼ teaspoon ground black pepper

Directions:
1. In a large bowl, combine the garlic, green onions, beans, jalapeno, red and yellow bell pepper, onion, cilantro and mix together well.
2. Add the lime zest and juice, Ro-tel, salt and pepper and mix. Adjust seasoning to your own taste.
3. Refrigerate for at one hour, minimum, before serving, so the flavors have time to blend. Serve with wheat tortilla slices that have been crisped in the oven or with wheat or sesame crackers.

Cannellini Bean Cashew Dip

This dip has a nutty flavor that adds to its character. I use whole-wheat crackers with the dip, but sometimes I just spread it on five-grain bread and eat it as a sandwich. Everything goes in a food processor and the end product is smooth and very creamy. Be sure not to "over-process," or it becomes a watery mess. It serves six to eight people.

Ingredients:
1 15-ounce can cannellini beans, rinsed and drained
½ cup raw cashews
1 clove garlic, smashed
2 tablespoons diced, red bell pepper
½ teaspoon sea salt
¼ teaspoon cayenne pepper
4 teaspoons lemon juice

2 tablespoons water
Dill sprigs or weed for garnish

Directions:

1. Place the beans, cashews, garlic and bell pepper in the food processor and pulse several times to break it up.
2. Add the salt, cayenne, lemon juice and water and process until smooth.
3. Scrape into a bowl, cover and refrigerate for at least an hour before serving.
4. Garnish with fresh dill and serve with vegetables, crackers or pita chips.

Cauliflower Popcorn

A Dehydrator Is A Handy Kitchen Appliance

This recipe is just plain fun. The cauliflower "is" the popcorn in this snack. A dehydrator is required to make this dish, but you can try to try them in a very low oven. My oven's lowest temperature is 150 degrees, Fahrenheit and it takes several hours for the cauliflower to dry out enough to be right. Drying it in a dehydrator works much better. This recipe makes about two cups.

Ingredients:
¼ cup sun-dried tomatoes
¾ cup dates
2 heads cauliflower
½ cup water
2 tablespoons raw tahini
1 tablespoon apple cider vinegar
2 teaspoons onion powder
2 teaspoons garlic powder
1 teaspoon ground cayenne pepper
2 tablespoons nutritional yeast (optional)

Directions:
1. Cover the sun-dried tomatoes warm water and let them soak for an hour.
2. If the dates are not soft and fresh, soak them in warm water for an hour in another bowl.
3. Cut the cauliflower in very small, bite-sized pieces then set aside.
4. Put the drained tomatoes and dates in a blender along with the water, tahini, apple cider vinegar, onion powder, garlic powder, cayenne pepper, nutritional yeast and turmeric. Blend into a thick, smooth consistency.
5. Pour this mixture into the bowl, atop the cauliflower and mix so that all the pieces are coated.
6. Place the cauliflower in the dehydrator and spread it out to make a single layer. Sprinkle with a little sea salt and set for 115 degrees, Fahrenheit for 12 to 24 hours or until it becomes exactly as crunchy as you like it. I let mine go for 15 to 16 hours, but the time will vary based on your taste preference as well as the ambient humidity.
7. Store in an airtight container until serving.

Cinnamon Apple Chips with Dip

Apple Chips Are Tasty And Healthier Than Potato Chips

This is a sweet treat of cinnamon dip; it tastes like a big cinnamon apple. The chips are made from apples soaked in lemon juice, so they don't turn an ugly brown. I use a mandolin to slice my apple chips thin, but you can cut them with a knife. If you do use a mandolin, leave the core intact and remove it after the slices are cut. You can cut them very thin that way so they will bend and won't break. The recipe makes about 40 chips and 2½ cups of dip.

Ingredients:
1 cup raw cashews
2 apples, thinly sliced
1 lemon
1½ cups water, divided
Cinnamon plus more to dust the chips
Another medium cored apple quartered
1 tablespoon honey or agave
1 teaspoon cinnamon
¼ teaspoon sea salt

Directions:
1. Place the cashews in a bowl of warm water, deep enough to cover them and let them soak overnight.

2. Preheat the oven to 200 degrees, Fahrenheit. Line two baking sheets with parchment paper.
3. Juice the lemon into a large glass bowl and add two cups of the water. Place the sliced apples in the water as you cut them and when done, swish them around and drain.
4. Spread the apple slices across the baking sheet in a single layer and sprinkle with a little cinnamon. Bake for 90 minutes.
5. Remove the slices from the oven and flip each of them over. Put them back in the oven and bake for another 90 minutes, or until they are crisp. Remember, they will get crisper as they cool.
6. While the apple slices are cooking, drain the cashews and put them in a blender, along with the quartered apple, the honey, a teaspoon of cinnamon and a half cup of the remaining water. Process until thick and creamy. I like to refrigerate my dip for about an hour to chill, before serve alongside the room temperature apple slices.

Crunchy Asparagus Spears

These crunchy treats will become a favorite snack at your house. They are flavorful because of the garlic powder, pepper and paprika. I serve lemon juice on the side for dipping to add some additional zing, but they are good without it. This makes four servings of three spears each. You might want to make more.

Ingredients:
1 bunch asparagus spears (about 12 spears)
¼ cup nutritional yeast
2 tablespoons hemp seeds
1 teaspoon garlic powder
¼ teaspoon paprika (or more if you like paprika)
⅛ teaspoon ground pepper
¼ cup whole-wheat breadcrumbs
Juice of ½ lemon

Directions:
1. Preheat the oven to 350 degrees, Fahrenheit. Line a baking sheet with parchment paper.
2. Wash the asparagus, snapping off the white part at the bottom. Save it for making vegetable stock.
3. Mix together the nutritional yeast, hemp seed, garlic powder, paprika, pepper and breadcrumbs.
4. Place asparagus spears on the baking sheets giving them a little room in between and sprinkle with the mixture in the bowl.
5. Bake for up to 25 minutes, until crispy.
6. Serve with lemon juice if desired.

Cucumber Bites with Chive and Sunflower Seeds

This recipe makes 50 yummy cucumber bites. It's perfect for a snack or a party appetizer. I like to peel the cucumber in vertical strips, so my slices have green and white striped edges.

Ingredients:
1 cup raw sunflower seed
½ teaspoon salt
½ cup chopped fresh chives
1 clove garlic, chopped
2 tablespoons red onion, minced
2 tablespoons lemon juice

½ cup water (might need more or less)
4 large cucumbers

Directions:
1. Place the sunflower seeds and salt in the food processor and process to a fine powder. It will take only about 10 seconds.
2. Add the chives, garlic, onion, lemon juice and water and process until creamy, scraping down the sides frequently. The mixture should be very creamy; if not, add a little more water.
3. Cut the cucumbers into 1½-inch coin-like pieces.
4. Spread a spoonful of the sunflower mixture on top and set on a platter. Sprinkle more chopped chives on top and refrigerate until ready to serve.

Garlicky Kale Chips

Kale Chips Are Crunchy And Healthy

Kale chips are easy to make; these are a little different from regular chips because they also have a garlic flavor. Make the garlic-infused oil several days before you plan to make the chips. The infused oil is good for anything that needs a bit of garlic flavoring.

Ingredients:
4 cloves garlic
1 cup olive oil
8 to 10 cups fresh kale, chopped
1 tablespoon of garlic-flavored olive oil
½ teaspoon garlic salt
½ teaspoon pepper
1 pinch red pepper flakes (optional)

Directions:
1. Peel and crush the garlic clove and place it in a small jar with a lid. Pour the olive oil over the top, cover tightly and shake. This will keep in the refrigerator for several days. When you're ready to use it, strain out the garlic and retain the oil.
2. Preheat the oven to 175 degrees, Fahrenheit.
3. Spread out the kale on a baking sheet and drizzle with the olive oil. Sprinkle with garlic salt, pepper and red pepper flakes.
4. Bake for an hour, remove from the oven and let the chips cool.
5. Store in an airtight container if you don't plan to eat them right away.

Hummus-stuffed Baby Potatoes

You will need a steamer basket in a saucepan of boiling water to make these little gems. You can prepare your own hummus (see the recipe in Chapter 11) or you can use the store-bought variety. This recipe makes 24 delicious miniature potato snacks.

Ingredients:
12 small red potatoes, walnut-sized or slightly larger
Hummus (See recipe, Chapter 11.)
2 green onions, thinly sliced
¼ teaspoon paprika, for garnish

Directions:

1. Place two to three inches of water in a saucepan, set a steamer inside and bring the water to a boil.
2. Place the whole potatoes in the steamer basket and steam for about 20 minutes or until soft. Keep the pan from boiling dry by adding additional hot water as needed.
3. Dump the potatoes into a colander and run cold water over them until they can be handled.
4. Cut each potato open and scoop out most of the pulp, leaving the skin and a thin layer of potato intact.
5. Mix the hummus with most of the green onions (keep enough for garnish) and spoon a little into the area where the potato has been scooped out.
6. Sprinkle each filled potato half with paprika and serve.

Homemade Trail Mix

Trail Mix Gives Both Quick And Sustained Energy

Ever since I was a little girl, my family has traditionally taken large bags of trail mix when we travel. I've found it filling and delicious; there are plenty of nuts, oats and dried fruit to keep me going and to stave off hunger in between rest stops.

I still take trail mix with me on road trips and I keep a bag of it at work. It still keeps me going until time for the next meal. You can deviate from this recipe and include any finger-type food you want.

Ingredients:

½ cup uncooked old-fashioned oatmeal
½ cup chopped dates
2 cups whole grain cereal
¼ cup raisins
¼ cup almonds
¼ cup walnuts

Directions:
1. Mix all the ingredients in a large bowl.
2. Place in an airtight container until ready to use.

Nut Butter Maple Dip

Use Peanut, Almond, or Cashew Butter For This Delicious Dip

I like to serve this dip with sliced apples or pears dipped in lemon juice, but you can also spread it on whole-wheat crackers for a sweet snack. It makes about six servings.

Ingredients:
½ tablespoon ground flaxseed
1 teaspoon ground cinnamon
½ tablespoon maple syrup
2 tablespoons cashew milk
¾ cups crunchy, unsweetened peanut butter (See recipe, Chapter 11.)

Directions:
1. In a bowl, combine the flaxseed, cinnamon, maple syrup, cashew milk and peanut butter.
2. Use a fork to mix everything in. I stir it like I'm scrambling eggs. The mixture should be creamy. If it's too runny, add a little more peanut butter; if it's too thick, add a little more cashew milk.
3. Refrigerate for about an hour, covered and serve.

Oven Baked Sesame Fries

Sesame Potato Wedges Make A Delicious Snack

This makes two to four servings of wedge fries that are very deliciously crunchy. I love the mix of sesame and potatoes, it's the potato starch that makes the wedges crispy, but it's optional. I prefer using sesame oil to emphasize the sesame flavor, but you may use sunflower oil if you wish.

Ingredients:
1 pound Yukon Gold potatoes, skins on and cut into wedges
2 tablespoons sesame seeds
1 tablespoon potato starch
1 tablespoon sesame oil
Salt to taste
Black pepper to taste

Directions:

1. Preheat the oven to 425 degrees, Fahrenheit and cover a baking sheet or two with parchment paper.
2. Cut the potatoes and place in a large bowl.
3. Add the sesame seeds, potato starch, sesame oil, salt and pepper.
4. Toss with your hands and make sure all the wedges are coated. Add more sesame seeds or oil if needed.
5. Spread the potato wedges on the baking sheets with some room between each wedge.
6. Bake for 15 minutes, flip the wedges over and then return them to the oven for 10 to 15 more minutes, until they look golden and crispy.

Pumpkin Orange Spice Hummus

Whole Chickpeas and Chopped Cilantro Make A Great Garnish

Hummus makes a good snack and there are a variety of ways to add punch and vary the flavor. This hummus adds a warm autumnal note. It keeps well in the refrigerator, up to a week. It tastes just as delicious served warm or cold. Dip into it with wheat crackers or pita chips. This recipe makes about four cups of hummus.

Ingredients:

1 cup canned, unsweetened pumpkin puree (See recipe, Chapter 11.)
1 16-ounce can garbanzo beans, rinsed and drained
1 tablespoon apple cider vinegar
1 tablespoon maple syrup
¼ cup tahini
1 tablespoon fresh orange juice
½ teaspoon orange zest and additional zest for garnish
⅛ teaspoon ground cinnamon
⅛ teaspoon ground ginger
⅛ teaspoon ground nutmeg
¼ teaspoon salt

Directions:
1. Pour the pumpkin puree and garbanzo beans into a food processor and pulse to break up.
2. Add the vinegar, syrup, tahini, orange juice and orange zest pulse a few times.
3. Add the cinnamon, ginger, nutmeg and salt and process until smooth and creamy.
4. Serve in a bowl sprinkled with more orange zest with wheat crackers alongside.

Quick English Muffin Mexican Pizzas

Half An English Muffin Makes A Good Pizza Base

My mother used to make mini English muffin pizzas for snacks. This is a plant-based Mexican version, which you can make yourself. The recipe yields four mini pizzas, so double or triple it as you wish. These pizzas also make excellent appetizers for a party.

Ingredients:
  2 whole-wheat English muffins separated
  ⅓ cup tomato salsa (See recipe, Chapter 11.)
  ¼ cup refried beans (See recipe, Chapter 11.)
  1 small jalapeno, seeded and sliced
  ¼ cup onion, sliced
  2 tablespoons diced plum or cherry tomato
  ⅓ cup vegan cheese shreds (pepper jack is really tasty!)

Directions:
  1. Preheat the oven to 400 degrees, Fahrenheit and cover a baking sheet with foil. The foil makes the crust crispier.
  2. Separate the English muffin and spread on some salsa and refried beans.

3. Place some of the jalapenos and onions on top and sprinkle the cheese over all.
4. Place on the baking sheet and bake for 10 to 15 minutes or until brown. You can turn on the broiler for a minute or two to melt the cheese.

Quinoa Trail Mix Cups

Loose trail mix can be messy, but this recipe contains them in muffin tins. They look like little cups when you are done and they stand up well to hikes, car trips, or about any place else but a swimming pool! This recipe makes 16 of the little cups and they stay fresh for about a week in an airtight container, but I doubt they'll be around that long.

Ingredients:
2 tablespoons ground flaxseed
⅓ cup unsweetened soy milk
1 cup old-fashioned rolled oats
1 cup cooked and cooled quinoa
¼ cup brown sugar
1 teaspoon ground cinnamon
¼ teaspoon salt
¼ cup pumpkin or sunflower seeds
¼ cup shredded coconut
½ cup almonds
½ cup raisins or dried cherries/cranberries

Directions:
1. Whisk the flaxseed and milk together in a small bowl and set aside for 10 minutes so the seed can absorb the milk.
2. Preheat the oven to 350 degrees, Fahrenheit and coat a muffin tin with coconut oil.
3. In a large bowl, mix the oats, quinoa, brown sugar, cinnamon, salt, pumpkin seeds, coconut, almonds and raisins.
4. Stir in the flaxseed and milk mixture and combine thoroughly.

5. Place two heaping teaspoons of the trail mix mixture in each muffin cup. When done, wet your fingers and press down on each muffin cup to compact the trail mix.
6. Bake for 12 minutes.
7. Cool completely before removing and each little cup will fall out. Store in an airtight container.

Sesame Potato Bites

Pop A Sesame Potato Bite Into Your Mouth And Enjoy

This is another recipe that combines sesame seeds with potatoes, but this time the shape is not wedges but little golf-ball-sized puffs. This recipe makes about 20 yummy bite-sized balls.

Ingredients:
4 medium sized russet potatoes, washed and chopped, but not peeled
3 tablespoons olive oil, divided
3 cloves garlic, diced
1 cup onion, chopped
Salt and pepper to taste
½ cup chickpea flour, more if needed (See recipe, Chapter 11.)
¾ teaspoon baking powder
¼ cup nutritional yeast
½ cup potato starch
1 teaspoon salt

1 teaspoon paprika

⅛ teaspoon cayenne pepper

1 teaspoon dried oregano

¼ cup fresh parsley, finely chopped

1½ cups sesame seeds, even more as needed

Directions:
1. Place the potato pieces in a pot with enough water to cover them and bring to a boil.
2. Boil until the potatoes are soft and good for mashing.
3. Drain the potatoes, return them to the pot and mash by hand.
4. Add two tablespoons of the olive oil, along with the salt and pepper to taste; stir to mix. If the results are too thick, add a little water until they become creamy, then set them aside to cool.
5. Place the remaining olive oil in a skillet over medium high heat; add the garlic and onion and sauté for about three minutes, until the onion is soft. Add to the potato mixture and stir to combine.
6. Preheat the oven to 400 degrees, Fahrenheit and when potatoes are cool enough to handle, add the chickpea flour, baking powder, nutritional yeast, potato starch, salt, paprika, cayenne pepper, oregano and parsley and mix well. You should now have a dough that is much thicker than ordinary mashed potatoes.
7. Form the dough into golf-ball-sized spheres and roll in the sesame seeds. Place on a baking sheet covered with parchment paper and press down to flatten the balls a little.
8. Bake for 15 minutes, remove from the oven and flip each ball over, then return to the oven and bake for 15 more minutes.
9. Let the bites cool before serving.

Spicy Fried Chickpeas

Fried Chickpeas Are Full Of Protein

When I watch television to relax, you'll often find me popping spicy fried chickpeas into my mouth instead of popcorn. This recipe makes them a little hotter than I like, so I reduce the amount of cayenne pepper. If you like them atomic, feel free to increase the spice to a whole teaspoon.

You may also flavor these any way you want. Sometimes I'll add little sea salt and paprika or some Italian Seasoning. You can be as creative as you want. This recipe makes six to eight servings.

Ingredients:
1 teaspoon cayenne pepper
2 teaspoons smoked paprika
6 tablespoons olive oil
2 15-ounce cans chickpeas, rinsed, drained and patted dry with a paper towel

Directions:
1. In a little bowl, mix the cayenne pepper and paprika and set aside.
2. Heat the olive oil in a skillet over medium heat and pour in one can of the chickpeas. Sauté the chickpeas until they are golden brown, about 15 minutes.

3. Pour them out on a plate covered by a paper towel to drain.
4. Place the other can of chickpeas in the oil and fry them until golden brown.
5. Pour the drained chickpeas into a bowl. Place the newly fried chickpeas on another clean paper towel to drain.
6. Once those chickpeas drain, add them to the bowl with the others and sprinkle with the cayenne and paprika mixture. Toss well and serve.

Squash Chips

Kabocha Squash, a.k.a., Japanese Pumpkin

Vegetable chips are a real treat in my house and these are particularly good. They are made from the kabocha squash. Always leave the skin of the squash on when slicing; that way the chips remain ridged and don't get mushy. Always use pink Himalayan salt to season them because it has a mild and different flavor that complements the squash. This squash will release water as it cooks, so you will not need to add any. If you want your chips extra crispy, place cooling racks on top of your baking sheets. This allows the liquid to drain off the chips. I have also successfully used acorn squash, so I suppose any other hard winter squash will also work. This recipe makes four servings of chips.

Ingredients:

1 medium Kabocha Squash

Himalayan pink salt to taste

1 tablespoon dried thyme leaves

Directions:

1. Preheat the oven to 400 degrees, Fahrenheit and either line two baking sheets with parchment or place cooling racks on top of the baking sheets.
2. Wash and cut open the squash. Scrape out the seeds, Cut into thin uniform slices with a mandolin or by hand.
3. Lay the squash slices on the baking sheet, with
4. Sprinkle with the salt and dried thyme.
5. Bake 20 minutes or until the chips are brown and crispy.

Sweet Strawberry Fruit Leather

Fruit leather does contain sugar, but not very much, considering the huge quantity of leather you get out of it. You can reduce the recipe by half if you're concerned about having too much on hand. The fruit leather will keep for about a week when stored in an airtight container.

Ingredients:

1½ pounds fresh strawberries

½ cup sugar

3 tablespoons lemon juice

2 pinches of salt

Directions:

1. Preheat the oven to 170 degrees, Fahrenheit.
2. Place a silicone mat over a cookie sheet (you will need more than one). If you do not have silicone mats on hand, you can use oiled parchment paper, but the leather may still manage to stick to it.
3. Place the strawberries in a blender in batches and process until smooth. Pour the liquefied strawberries into a bowl.

4. Add the sugar, lemon juice and salt and stir to thoroughly combine.
5. Spread the mixture over the silicone sheet, leaving a space on each side so the leather is easily pulled off the mat when done.
6. Place the baking sheets in the oven and watch. The leather cooks slowly. The cooking process can take up to three hours. The mixture will be thick and pliable but will stick together and pull up from the pan. Let it cool before trying to pull it up or you will burn your fingers.
7. Pull up the sheet of fruit leather and place it on a cutting board. Use a pizza cutter to cut strips and place on a piece of parchment paper that is a little wider and longer than the strip. Roll the leather up along with the parchment paper.
8. Store your fruit leather in an airtight container until ready to eat.

Zucchini Chips

Zucchini Chips Are Delicious With A Sandwich Or With Dip

These are my favorite vegetable chips. Zucchini is always plentiful and they are easy to make. This recipe flavors the chips with paprika, salt and pepper, but you can also try dried thyme, basil, garlic powder, marjoram, or even a little cinnamon and sugar. This recipe makes two servings of chips that can be eaten as they

230

are or dipped in barbeque sauce or ranch dressing (both recipes are found in Chapter 11).

Ingredients:
   1 medium zucchini, thinly sliced with skin on
   1 tablespoon olive oil
   1 teaspoon salt
   ¼ teaspoon pepper
   ¾ teaspoon paprika

Directions:
   1. Preheat the oven to 400 degrees, Fahrenheit and prepare two baking sheets with parchment paper.
   2. Place the slices of zucchini on the baking sheets and make sure they are not touching.
   3. Brush lightly with olive oil.
   4. Mix the salt, pepper and paprika in a small bowl, whisking it together. Sprinkle on the zucchini chips.
   5. Place in the oven and bake for 10 minutes. Rotate the pan and bake for 15 more minutes, watching to ensure that they don't scorch or turn too brown.
   6. Let the chips cool for five minutes before serving.

The next chapter will give you oodles of recipes for sweet treats and desserts. Some use sugar, but most of the recipes use honey, agave, or maple syrup as sweeteners.

Chapter 10: Deserts You Can Feel Great About

Everyone deserves a bit of a sweet treat occasionally. All the recipes in this chapter are plant-based and they avoid refined sugar, preferring sweeteners like agave, honey and maple syrup. Some still contain plenty of calories, so be forewarned. These recipes include cakes, brownies, mousse, ice pops and more.

Avocado-based Chocolate Mousse

Garnish With Blueberries, Strawberries, Or A Mint Leaf

You'll use avocados and agave to make this elegant chocolate mousse. You may wish to experiment with maple syrup instead of the agave for a different flavor. When it's frozen, this mousse can become a lovely ice cream. It makes four servings. Try serving it with sliced strawberries on top.

Please note that the cacao in the ingredients is not a misspelling of the word "cocoa" Cacao is a less-processed version of cocoa bean powder; consequently it contains more nutrients, fewer toxic chemicals and is easier to digest than its similarly-spelled cousin.

Ingredients:
4 ripe avocados
1 cup agave syrup, divided

1 cup cacao, divided
¼ teaspoon salt
¼ teaspoon vanilla extract (See recipe, Chapter 11.)

Directions:
1. Prepare the avocados and place the meat in a food processor. Process until smooth.
2. Add half the agave syrup, half the cacao, the salt and the vanilla; process until smooth.
3. Taste to see if it needs more agave syrup or cacao and add anything that's lacking.
4. Refrigerate for at least two hours, or overnight, before serving.

Banana Creamy Pie

Banana cream pie is difficult for me to pass up, but I have a little less guilt eating this one. It is sweetened using coconut sugar, so it'll have the calories, but not the bad stuff that goes with refined sugar.

Ingredients:
2 large pitted dates (soaked in warm water for about one hour)
1 pre-made pie crust, cooled (See the recipe in Chapter 11.)
2 very ripe bananas, peeled and sliced, plus one a little less ripe for garnish
1 tablespoon coconut sugar
1 can coconut milk
½ teaspoon vanilla (See recipe, Chapter 11.)
1 pinch salt

Directions:
1. Soak the dates for about an hour, then drain and dry them.
2. Place the dates and banana slices in a food processor and pulse to break them up.
3. Add the coconut sugar, coconut milk, vanilla and salt and process until smooth and creamy.

4. Pour the filling into a cooled pie crust. It must be cool, or it will make the crust soggy.
5. Cover with plastic wrap and place the pie in the freezer for at least two hours.
6. Remove from the freezer and let it thaw a bit. Slice the remaining banana and place it on top. Serve while still partially frozen.

Banana Mango Ice Cream

This recipe is a tropical, refreshing and sweet treat. If you prefer a little more sweetness than provided by the banana or mangos, just add some stevia or agave syrup. The recipe makes two servings of delicious tropical ice cream.

Ingredients:
1 banana, peeled and sliced
2 ripe mangos with the skin removed and the flesh cubed
3 tablespoons almond or cashew milk, chilled (coconut milk also works well)

Directions:
1. Lay out the banana and mango slices on a baking sheet lined with parchment paper and place them in the freezer.
2. Once they are frozen solid, remove the fruit and place it in the food processor.
3. Add the cold milk and process until smooth, about three to four minutes.
4. Taste and add sweetener as needed.
5. Serve immediately.

Berry Chia Jam Thumbprint Cookies

Thumbprint Cookies Aren't Just For the Holidays Anymore

I remember thumbprint cookies my mom used to make. Here is a gluten-free and plant-based version using berry chia jam that you make yourself. The first part of the recipe consists of how to make the jam and the second part will instruct you on preparing the cookies. With the jam, you have some options. You can use either fresh or frozen berries and you can use strawberries, raspberries, blackberries or any berry you like. The sweetener called for is maple syrup, but you can substitute a half teaspoon of liquid Stevia instead, if you prefer. This recipe makes about 18 cookies.

Ingredients for Jam:
   16 ounces fresh berries or a bag of frozen berries, defrosted
   6 tablespoons chia seeds
   1 tablespoon fresh lemon juice
   2 to 3 tablespoon maple syrup

Directions for Jam:
   1. Remove stems or pits (cherries can also be used) and roughly chop the fruit.

2. Place the fruit in a saucepan over medium heat until it starts to break down and become watery. Remove from the heat.
3. Use a potato masher to mash the fruit.
4. Add the chia seeds, lemon juice and the syrup; stir well.
5. Pour into a bowl, cover with plastic wrap and place in the refrigerator until it thickens, at least two hours, but possibly overnight as well. If it doesn't thicken enough add a few more chia seeds and refrigerate a little longer.

Ingredients for Cookies:
1¼ cups oat flour (See the recipe in Chapter 11)
1½ cups almond flour
½ teaspoon salt
½ teaspoon ground cinnamon
⅓ cup maple syrup
⅓ cup coconut oil
Berry chia jam

Directions for Cookies:
1. Preheat oven to 350 degrees, Fahrenheit and line cookie sheets with parchment paper.
2. In a bowl, whisk together the oat flour and almond flour, the cinnamon and the salt until well combined.
3. In another bowl, whisk the maple syrup and coconut oil.
4. Take a handheld rotary mixer and add a little of the dry ingredients to the maple syrup ingredients. Keep adding gradually until it is all combined. It should look like a soft cookie dough.
5. Scoop the dough out by teaspoonfuls and roll into a ball. Place on the cookie sheet about a half to one inch apart and make an indentation with the back of a spoon (or your thumb) in the middle of the cookie.
6. Place in the oven and bake for eight minutes, then rotate the baking sheets and bake for another seven minutes or until the cookies are golden brown.
7. Remove from oven and place a spoonful of jam in each cookie's indentation.

8. Return to the oven for two to three minutes; then remove to cool completely.
9. Store in an airtight container.

Cardamom Baked Pears

I always think of cardamom as an exotic spice because its flavor is like nothing else on earth. Pears have a mild flavor but when you combine them with cardamom they give you a succulent treat. This recipe makes two servings.

Ingredients:
¼ cup white wine
1 teaspoon vanilla (See recipe, Chapter 11.)
½ teaspoon ground cardamom
2 to 4 firm ripe pears, halved and cored
1½ tablespoons lemon juice
2 tablespoons sugar

Directions:
1. Preheat the oven to 400 degrees, Fahrenheit.
2. Whisk together the wine, vanilla and cardamom in an 8 by 8 inch square baking dish.
3. Set the pears in the baking dish with the cut side up. Drizzle the lemon juice over them. This will prevent the pears from turning an ugly brown.
4. Sprinkle with the sugar.
5. Cover the pan with foil and bake for 30 minutes.
6. Remove the foil and prick with a fork to see if the pears are tender. If not, return to the oven for five more minutes.
7. Place the pears in two bowls and drizzle with the sauce in the bottom of the pan.

Cashew Cream Baked Apples

Sweet Baked Apples; Just Add The Cashew Cream On Top

This is a plant-based version of baked apples using maple syrup to sweeten and cashews to add a nutty flavor. It makes four simply delicious servings that are sweet and creamy.

Ingredients:

   1 cup raw cashews
   4 large apples
   Coconut oil for greasing the pan
   ¾ cup water, divided
   ½ teaspoon vanilla (See recipe, Chapter 11.)
   3 tablespoons maple syrup, divided
   ½ teaspoon ground cinnamon
   ⅓ cup favorite nuts or ¼ cup granola

Directions:

1. Soak the cashews for at least one hour in enough hot water to cover them.
2. Preheat the oven to 400 degrees, Fahrenheit.

3. Core the apples and peel a strip of skin off the top and bottom of each apple. Carefully cut the bottoms flat. Coat an 8 or 9-inch square baking dish with coconut oil and place the apples in the bottom of the pan.
4. Drain the cashews and put them in a blender, along with a half cup of water, two tablespoons of maple syrup and the vanilla; blend until smooth. This might take a few minutes.
5. Pour the mixture into a bowl, cover it and place it in the refrigerator while the apples bake.
6. Place the nuts or granola in the apple core hole.
7. Drizzle the apples with the remaining tablespoon of maple syrup and sprinkle with cinnamon.
8. Pour a quarter cup of water into the bottom of the baking dish and cover it. Bake for 30 to 45 minutes.
9. Check at 30 minutes by uncovering the dish and poking the apples. If they are soft, they are done; if not cover the dish again and let them continue baking up to the 45 minute mark.
10. Remove the dish from the oven, remove the covering and let cool for about 10 minutes.
11. Place in individual bowls and top with the cashew cream.

Chickpea Chocolate Chip Peanut Butter Cookies

Peanut Butter Cookies Made From Chickpeas

These cookies taste like regular peanut butter chocolate chip cookies without the flour and sugar. Instead the cookies are made out of chickpeas and maple syrup. The recipe makes a dozen cookies. I'll warn you now. You won't be able to stop at just one.

Ingredients:
½ cup smooth peanut butter (See recipe, Chapter 11.)
1 15-ounce can chickpeas, rinsed and drained
⅓ cup maple syrup
1 teaspoon vanilla (See recipe, Chapter 11.)
⅓ cup old-fashioned rolled oats
1 teaspoon baking soda
¼ teaspoon salt (only if the peanut butter isn't already salted)
½ cup chocolate chips
¼ cup chopped walnuts (optional)

Directions:
1. Preheat the oven to 350 degrees, Fahrenheit and cover baking sheets with parchment paper.
2. Place the peanut butter, chickpeas, maple syrup and vanilla in a food processor and continue to process until smooth.
3. In a bowl, whisk together the rolled oats, baking soda and salt (optional). Gradually add this mixture to the ingredients in the food processor, to make a dough.
4. Remove the dough to a bowl and add the chocolate chips and walnuts; stir by hand to mix.
5. Scoop out by heaping teaspoonfuls and space them apart on the baking sheets. Crisscross the mounds lightly with a fork.
6. Bake for 10 to 15 minutes, until the cookies turn golden brown.
7. Cool on baking sheets for five minutes before transferring to cooling racks.

Dairy-free Mango Chia Seed Parfaits

Mango Chia Seed Parfaits Are Pretty, Elegant, Light and Fresh

You'll want to layer this parfait in clear, tall glass dishes or glasses to show them off. I put mine in a glass jar with a lid, so I can carry it with me for lunch. When soaked in liquid, chia seeds expand and create a delicious, sticky-sweet substance perfect for a parfait. This recipe makes two to four servings

Ingredients:

½ cup chia seeds
2 cups coconut milk
1 teaspoon vanilla extract (See recipe, Chapter 11.)
¼ teaspoon cardamom
2 tablespoons date paste
1 medium mango

Directions:

1. Pour the chia seeds in a bowl with the coconut milk.
2. Add the vanilla, cardamom and date paste and mix well. Cover and refrigerate overnight.
3. Skin the mango and cut off the flesh in chunks, dropping them into a blender. Process until smooth.

4. Layer in your serving dishes the chia seed mixture, followed by the mango sauce.
5. Refrigerate for at least half an hour before serving.

Easy Tropical Ambrosia

The standard ambrosia recipe is made with fruit, coconut and marshmallows. This version is just as tasty, but it is plant-based and much healthier than the original. It is sweetened with maple syrup and is dairy-free. This recipe yields four servings.

Ingredients:
1 pack of soft silken tofu
1 teaspoon vanilla extract (See recipe, Chapter 11.)
½ can coconut milk
2 tablespoons maple syrup
3 tablespoons orange juice
1 large sweet apple, cored and chopped into small pieces
1 cup fresh pineapple, chopped
½ cup raw cashews, chopped (keep a little for garnish)
¼ cup shredded coconut (keep a little for garnish)

Directions:
1. Place the tofu in a blender along with the vanilla, coconut milk, maple syrup and orange juice; blend until smooth.
2. In a bowl, combine the apple, pineapple, most of the cashews and most of the coconut.
3. Pour the blender mixture atop the fruit and gently fold it in, so as not to damage the fruit..
4. Divide the ambrosia into four bowls and sprinkle with the reserved nuts and coconut before serving.

Key Lime Pie with Macadamia Nuts

The Macadamia Nut Crust Makes This Pie Special

The crust of this pie is included in this recipe and it contains dates, pecans and macadamia nuts. There is no flour and is also gluten free. The filling is made with avocados and it does not taste like avocados at all. The creamy texture comes from coconut milk and the tangy flavor derives from the lime juice. It is made in a 9-inch springform pan.

Ingredients:
½ cup dried pitted dates, soaked in water for at least an hour
1¼ cups pecans
1¼ cups macadamia nuts
¼ cup plus 1 pinch of salt, divided
2¼ teaspoons vanilla, divided (See recipe, Chapter 11.)
2 ripe avocados, halved, pitted and peeled
½ cup full-fat coconut milk
1 cup agave syrup
1¼ cups coconut oil
1½ cups fresh-squeezed lime juice (10 to 12 limes)

Directions:
1. Soak the dates for about an hour in enough water to cover them; drain well.

2. Grease a 9-inch springform pan with coconut oil and set aside.
3. Place the dates in a food processor along with the pecans, macadamia nuts, pinch of salt and a quarter teaspoon of the vanilla. Process until a workable dough is formed. Press this dough into the bottom of the springform pan and prick with a fork.
4. Process the avocado, coconut milk, agave syrup, remaining vanilla, coconut oil and lime juice; process until smooth and creamy.
5. Pour the filling into the crust, cover the pan and freeze overnight.
6. Thaw for two hours before serving.

Lemony Coconut Bars

Lemon Bars Go Great With Lemon Tea

No baking is required for these bar cookies. You just press the dough into an 8 by 8-inch pan and refrigerate for a few hours. They are ready to be cut and enjoyed.

Ingredients:

1 cup old-fashioned rolled oats
1½ cup unsweetened shredded coconut
2 tablespoons agave syrup
1 teaspoon vanilla extract (See recipe, Chapter 11.)
2 tablespoons coconut oil

244

½ cup oat flour (See recipe, Chapter 11)
1 lemon

Directions:

1. Place the rolled oats in a food processor and pulse a few times, to grind them finely. Pour this into a mixing bowl.
2. Place the coconut in the food processor and pulse until it is mealy. Pour into the bowl with the oats.
3. Add the agave syrup, vanilla, coconut oil and oat flour; stir to mix.
4. Zest the lemon into the bowl.
5. Cut the lemon in half and squeeze both halves into the bowl.
6. Stir well. You should have a thick dough-like substance.
7. Press into a pan that has been lined with parchment paper. Refrigerate it for about two hours, until the mixture becomes slightly hardened. Cut into squares and serve.

Miniature Fruit Cheesecakes

Now you can make plant-based individual cheesecakes! You'll use a muffin tin, lined with cupcake papers. The recipe makes 12 little perfectly-sized cheesecakes.

Ingredients:

2 cups raw cashews soaked overnight in enough water to cover them
3 tablespoons old-fashioned rolled oats
1 cup pecans
1 tablespoon ground flaxseed
3 large dates with pits removed
½ teaspoon seal salt
1½ large lemons, both the zest and the juice
1 tablespoon coconut oil, melted
2 tablespoons maple syrup
1 tablespoon unsweetened almond milk
Fresh blueberries or raspberries for garnish

Directions:

1. Place the cashews in a bowl and cover with water. Cover with plastic wrap and set aside overnight.
2. Prepare a 12-hole muffin tin, placing cupcake liners in each hole.
3. In a food processor, place the oats, pecans, flaxseed, dates and salt; process until it forms a sticky dough.
4. Drop a level tablespoon of dough into the bottom of each cupcake liner and press down. Set the muffin tin aside.
5. Drain and rinse the cashews and put them in a high speed blender. Pulse to break them up. Add the juice from one lemon and the zest from that lemon. Save the zest from the half lemon for later. Add the coconut oil, maple syrup and almond milk; blend for about 90 seconds. Scrape down the sides and blend again until the mixture is thoroughly combined and looks smooth and creamy.
6. Use 1½ teaspoons of filling to complete each mini-cheesecake. Sprinkle with lemon zest and place a berry on top.
7. Refrigerate at least three hours before serving.

Minty Chocolate Chip Truffles

Dust Truffles With A Little Cacao Powder

These truffles are great for the holidays, but I make them other times of the year as well. Note: I prefer to use vanilla extract instead of the peppermint flavoring.

This elegant dessert is easy enough to make; there's no baking required. You can stir these up by hand, but I find a mixer makes the work easier, at least until it's time to stir in the chocolate chips.

Ingredients:

2 tablespoons peanut butter (See recipe, Chapter 11.)
1 tablespoon unsweetened applesauce (See recipe, Chapter 11)
1 teaspoon agave syrup
1 cup almond flour
1 teaspoon peppermint or vanilla extract (See recipe, Chapter 11.)
3 tablespoons mini chocolate chips
Cacao powder for dusting

Directions:

1. Place the peanut butter, applesauce and agave syrup in a mixing bowl; combine with a mixer.
2. Add the flour, about a quarter cup at a time and combine well.
3. Mix in the extract.
4. Stir in the chocolate chips by hand.
5. Roll the dough into about 12 one-inch balls and roll them in cacao powder to prevent stickiness. I like to refrigerate them for about an hour before serving.
6. They will keep well for three to five days refrigerated in an airtight container, that is, if they aren't devoured immediately.

No-bake Chocoholic Pie

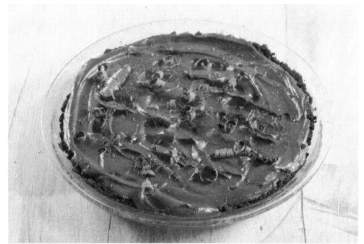

Use Only Silken Tofu To Make This Chocolate Pie

This pie is a real show stopper. I make a vegan graham cracker crust found in chapter 11, but you can also use the flaxseed baked crust, also found in chapter 11. You'll find this pie is chocolatey delicious. No one will ever guess the main ingredient is tofu.

Ingredients:
 1 premade pie crust
 1 pound silken tofu
 3 tablespoons maple syrup
 1 cup full-fat coconut milk
 1 teaspoon vanilla extract (See recipe, Chapter 11.)
 ½ teaspoon salt
 ⅔ cup nondairy chocolate chips, melted

Directions:
 1. Place the tofu in a blender and pulse to break it up.
 2. Add the maple syrup, coconut milk, vanilla and salt, blending until smooth.
 3. Remove one cup of the mixture for later.
 4. Add the melted chocolate chips and blend them in well.
 5. Pour the mixture from the blender into the prepared pie crust.

6. Pour a cup of the non-chocolate mixture on top and spread it out carefully. Take a butter knife and swirl it around to bring up some of the chocolate-infused mixture and create beautiful designs on top of the pie.
7. Refrigerate for at least two hours before serving.

No-bake Peanut Butter Chocolate Balls

No-bake cookies are fun to make. This recipe is sweetened with dates. You can use vegan chocolate chips to avoid refined sugars, but remember that chocolate is a plant too. This recipe makes 12 to 15 balls.

Ingredients:
1 cup pitted dates
¾ cups old-fashioned rolled oats
3 tablespoons peanut butter (See recipe, Chapter 11.)
¼ cup chocolate chips

Directions:
1. Place the dates in a bowl and cover them with warm water. Soak for about 15 minutes.
2. Drain the dates and use your hands to squeeze out any excess water; dry the dates on clean paper towels.
3. Place the dates in a food processor and roughly chop them.
4. Add the oats and peanut butter and pulse to form a sticky dough. Pour the dough into a bowl.
5. Fold in the chocolate chips and shape dough pieces into balls. Place them on a baking sheet lined with either wax paper or parchment paper. Refrigerate the balls for a few hours before serving.
6. Store in an airtight container in the refrigerator.

No-bake Pecan Apricot Balls

These Cookies Can Be Popped Right Into Your Mouth

These no-bake cookies are fruity and delicious with dried apricots as the star of the show. This recipe will make a dozen cookies.

Ingredients:
1 cup dried apricots
½ cup pecans
1 teaspoon vanilla extract (See recipe, Chapter 11.)
½ cup old-fashioned rolled oats
½ cup shredded coconut (optional)

Directions:
1. Place apricots in a food processor and pulse to chop until they are mealy.
2. Add the pecans and chop on high for about 20 seconds.
3. Add the vanilla and oats and process to a smooth dough, about 20 more seconds.
4. Scoop the dough by tablespoons and form into balls. Roll each ball in the coconut and place on a baking sheet lined with wax paper or parchment paper.
5. Refrigerate the balls for about two hours. After serving, store any leftovers in the refrigerator in an airtight container.

No-bake Pistachio Balls

This no-bake cookie recipe only has three ingredients but they pack a punch. Pistachios are green, so I dye my shredded coconut green by placing in a glass jar with a lid, dropping in some liquid food coloring and shaking until the coconut turns green. I open the lid and spread it out on parchment paper to let it dry for about 15 minutes. Otherwise your fingers turn green when you roll the cookies in the coconut. This recipe makes one dozen cookies.

Ingredients:
   ½ cup pistachio nuts, no shells
   1 cup pitted dates
   2 tablespoons coconut

Directions:
   1. Place the pistachios in a food processor and chop well.
   2. Add the dates and process until a dough forms.
   3. Scoop out two tablespoons to make one ball, roll it in the coconut and place on baking sheet that's been lined with wax paper or parchment paper.
   4. Refrigerate the sheet-full of cookies for about an hour before serving. Store any leftover cookies in an airtight container in the refrigerator.

Peach Crisp with Date Sugar

Throw Blueberries On Top Before Cooking For a Tasty Treat

Date sugar is made from dehydrated dates that have been ground up. The only real problem with this form of sweetness is that it won't dissolve all the way, as with regular sugar. However, this is one of the healthiest sugars to use. Date sugar is quite expensive, but it's worth the price for special occasions.

This recipe only uses a few tablespoons of date sugar, with the peaches and a half cup in the topping. You can make your own oat flour by grinding the rolled oats (see chapter 11 for a recipe) and include use some whole rolled oats as well. My grandmother always made peach crisp during peach season and this tastes much like hers. It makes six servings.

Ingredients:
    5 to 6 large peaches, peeled and sliced
    3 tablespoons chia seeds
    1 tablespoon lemon juice
    3 teaspoons ground cinnamon, divided
    ⅛ cup date sugar
    ¼ cup oat flour
    1 cup old-fashioned oats
    ½ additional cup date sugar
    1 tablespoon maple syrup
    ⅛ teaspoon ground nutmeg

3 heaping tablespoons of smooth almond butter (See recipe, Chapter 11.)

Directions:
1. Peel and cut the peaches putting them in a bowl and sprinkle the chia seeds, lemon juice, two teaspoons of the cinnamon and the eighth cup of date sugar over the top. Give it a stir, taste to make sure it is sweet enough and set aside for 15 minutes so the chia seeds can thicken up.
2. Preheat the oven to 350 degrees, Fahrenheit.
3. Pour the peaches into the bottom of a nonstick sprayed 8½ by 11 inch baking dish and set aside.
4. In a bowl, prepare the topping by adding together the oat flour, rolled oats, half-cup of date sugar, maple syrup, the remaining teaspoon of cinnamon, the nutmeg and the almond butter and mixing well. It should have a crumbly consistency.
5. Sprinkle the crumb mixture on top of the peaches.
6. Bake for 30 minutes or until the topping browns. Let it cool for 10 minutes before serving.

Pumpkin Oatmeal Cookies

Pumpkin Cookies Make The Whole House Smell Like Fall

Here's another recipe that uses our old friend, oat flour. You can make your own, using the instructions in chapter 11.

These cookies are soft and delicious, while also spicy with a hint of autumn. I often add a half cup of golden raisins to the batter, but this is purely an option. If you want to try to make your own pumpkin puree from a pumpkin, I have put a recipe in chapter 11 as well. This recipe makes 32 cookies.

Ingredients:
    1 cup oat flour (See recipe, Chapter 11)
    2 cups old-fashioned rolled oats
    1 cup sugar or ½ cup date sugar
    1 teaspoon baking soda
    ¼ teaspoon nutmeg
    1 teaspoon cinnamon
    ⅛ teaspoon salt
    1 15-ounce can pumpkin puree (See Chapter 11 for a recipe)
    ¼ cup vanilla almond milk

½ cup golden raisins (optional)

Directions:
1. Preheat the oven to 35 degrees, Fahrenheit and cover two baking sheets with parchment paper.
2. Place the oat flour, rolled outs, sugar, baking soda, nutmeg, cinnamon and salt in a large mixing bowl and stir together.
3. Combine the puree and the almond milk and whisk together.
4. Pour the pumpkin puree mixture into the dry mixture, stirring well with a wooden spoon after each addition. Once it is well mixed, add the raisins if you are going to use them.
5. Scoop the batter out, a heaping tablespoon at a time and roll it into a ball. Space these balls apart evenly on the baking sheets.
6. Flatten each ball lightly with a fork.
7. Bake for 24 to 28 minutes, until brown. Let the cookies cool for five minutes before transferring them to cooling racks.

Raspberry Fudge Tart

This is a fancy dessert suitable for company. Chickpeas are the ingredient that gives this tart some texture, but don't worry; your tart will taste like chocolate, not chickpeas. This recipe yields eight servings.

Ingredients for crust:
2 cups old-fashioned rolled oats
1 tablespoon coconut sugar
4 tablespoons cocoa
¼ cup coconut oil
¼ teaspoon salt
5 to 7 tablespoons cold water

Ingredients for filling:
2 cups canned chickpeas, rinsed and drained well

2 tablespoons coconut oil
5 tablespoons cocoa
½ cup semi-sweet dark chocolate chips
½ teaspoon salt
6 tablespoons maple syrup
1 tablespoon vanilla extract (See recipe, Chapter 11.)
4 tablespoons almond milk
1 large container of fresh raspberries

Directions:

1. Preheat the oven to 350 degrees, Fahrenheit and coat a tart pan with nonstick spray, then set aside.
2. Place the oats in a food processor or blender and process until they become a coarse flour.
3. Add the coconut sugar, cocoa, coconut oil and salt; process until combined.
4. Gradually add the water, one tablespoon at a time. Check after the third tablespoon. If the dough sticks together when you squeeze it with your hands, it is ready. If not, keep adding water until it does.
5. Press the dough into the tart pan on the bottom and up the sides evenly; prick the dough with a fork.
6. Take a piece of parchment paper and set it on top of the crust. Pour dried beans on top of the parchment paper to weight down the crust. Bake it for 25 minutes.
7. Remove the beans and the paper, then return the crust to the oven for 10 more minutes. Remove it and wait until the crust is completely cool before adding the filling.
8. Place the rinsed and drained chickpeas in the food processor and pulse to break them up.
9. Add the coconut oil, cocoa, chocolate chips, salt, maple syrup, vanilla and milk; process until smooth.
10. Pour this mixture into the crust and top with raspberries.
11. Place in the refrigerator for at least two hours before serving.

Strawberry Pie with Walnut Crust

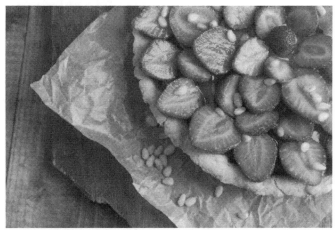

Fresh Strawberry Pie Is Delightfully Refreshing

This walnut crust is so good you will want to use it for other types of pie, including peach. The filling calls for turbinado sugar. This sugar does come from sugar cane, which is a plant, but refined sugar comes from the same place. Turbinado sugar, however, comes from the first pressing of the cane, so it retains more of the original molasses flavor then does refined sugar. If you would rather use agave syrup for your sweetener, use three tablespoons instead.

The crust is made by mixing oat flour and walnuts. This recipe makes a single pie that can be cut into six or eight slices.

Ingredients:
¾ cup raw walnuts
1 cup oat flour (See recipe, Chapter 11)
¾ cups rolled oats
¼ teaspoon Himalayan salt (optional: substitute regular table salt)
3 tablespoons maple syrup
¼ cup coconut oil, melted
2½ pounds fresh strawberries, divided
2 tablespoons cornstarch
¼ cup water
½ cup apple juice

3 tablespoons turbinado sugar

Directions:
1. Preheat oven to 350 degrees, Fahrenheit and coat a deep dish pie pan with nonstick spray.
2. Place the walnuts in the food processor and pulse until they are roughly chopped with no large chunks.
3. Add the oat flour, the rolled oats, salt, maple syrup and melted coconut oil; pulse until everything is well combined.
4. Pour the mixture into the pie pan and gently press it down on the bottom and up the sides.
5. Bake the crust for 10 to 15 minutes or until the edges brown. Remove from the oven and set the pan on a cooling rack.
6. Take six strawberries and remove the stems. Put them in a blender and liquefy them. Pour into a quarter-cup measuring cup and if you do not have enough to make a fourth of a cup, liquefy a few more until you do. If you have a little more than a fourth cup, it will not matter. Pour this strawberry puree into a small saucepan.
7. In a small bowl, combine the cornstarch and the water. Stir until the cornstarch is dissolved.
8. Place the saucepan over medium heat and add the apple juice and the sugar. Whisk well and bring the contents to a simmer.
9. Once it starts to boil, reduce the heat to a simmer and whisk constantly until it turns shiny and thickens to form a glaze. Remove from the heat and set aside.
10. Hull and slice the rest of the strawberries into a bowl and pour the glaze over the top. Gently fold the glaze in and pour it all into the baked pie crust.
11. Refrigerate for 45 minutes to an hour before slicing and serving.

Sunny Mango Lime Ice Pops

Mangos Make For Sunny Tropical Ice Pops Fit For A King

I wanted to include this ice pop recipe, because it appeals to both adults and kids. Regular mangos will turn the pops orange, but if you can find yellow mangos, they will give you some neon yellow goodies.

Mango is already tropically refreshing on a hot day but in the frozen form it can't be beat. This recipe yields four luscious mango lime pops.

Ingredients:
2 yellow mangos, peeled and flesh removed
1 lime (both juice and zest)
¼ cup coconut water
2 packets of stevia

Directions:
1. Roughly chop the mango flesh and put it in a blender.
2. Scrape the zest from the lime and put it in the blender, too. Cut the lime in half, remove seeds and squeeze the juice into a half-cup measuring cup.
3. Add enough coconut water to the measuring cup to make a full half cup.

4. Place the coconut water and lime juice combination in the blender along with the stevia.
5. Blend on high until smooth.
6. Pour into molds and freeze.
7. If you don't have molds, you can appropriate some small paper cups, filling them with the ingredients and putting them in the freezer for up to an hour. Before they are completely frozen, poke a popsicle stick into the center so it will stand up straight.
8. To remove, run warm water over the molds. You can tear off the paper cups to make this kind of popsicle accessible.

Sweet Potato Brownies

Sweet Potato Brownies Actually Taste Better

Yes, you can make brownies with sweet potatoes. In fact, the sweet potatoes add a nice moist texture to the brownies while lending their sweetness to the dessert. This recipe calls for almond meal and oat flour; the latter you can make your own oat flour by following the recipe in Chapter 11.

The brownies will be very dense. They remind me of a mix between a brownie and fudge. Chocolate lovers will flock to this dessert. You'll get 12 servings from this recipe.

Ingredients:

1 pound sweet potatoes
½ cup almond meal
½ cup oat flour (See recipe, Chapter 11)
10 tablespoons cacao powder
½ cup maple syrup
1 to 6 teaspoons almond milk
⅓ cup dark chocolate chips
½ cup creamy nut butter (optional)

Directions:

1. Roast the sweet potatoes in the oven and peel off the skins once they are cool enough to handle.
2. Cut the sweet potatoes in chunks and put in a food processor. Process until they are smooth.
3. Preheat the oven to 350 degrees, Fahrenheit and spray an 8 by 8-inch baking pan with nonstick spray.
4. Add the almond meal, oat flour, cacao powder and maple syrup to the food process and process. The batter should be thick like a cross between cookie and cake batter. If it is too thick (it probably will be) add one to six teaspoons almond milk until you reach the correct consistency. If it is too thin, add a little more oat flour. Pour the batter into a bowl.
5. Fold in the chocolate chips by hand.
6. Pour the batter into the prepared pan and bake for 25 to 30 minutes or until firm.
7. If you are going to use the nut butter, pull the pan out of the oven and immediately spread the nut butter over the entire surface so it melts into the brownies.
8. Let the brownies cool completely. Cut into 12 servings and place in an airtight container. Store any leftovers in the refrigerator.

Yummy Apple Nachos

Sweet Caramel Sauce & The Tartness Of A Granny Smith Apple

This is a fun snack that anyone will enjoy and it is very easy to make. I have split the ingredients and directions into several sections to make it easy to follow. This recipe should serve four people.

Ingredients – Caramel Sauce
½ cup pitted dates
¼ teaspoon vanilla bean powder
¼ teaspoon ground cinnamon
¼ teaspoon ground nutmeg
¼ teaspoon sea salt
⅛ teaspoon ground allspice
⅓ cup water

Ingredients – Apple Base
3 apples, cored and sliced (if the skin is too thick, peel it and discard)
2 teaspoons lemon juice

Ingredients – Toppings (use 1 or 2)
3 to 4 tablespoons nut butter
2 to 3 tablespoons dried cranberries or raisins
2 to 3 tablespoons chopped nuts

1½ to 2 cups popped popcorn
3 to 4 tablespoons chocolate chips
2 tablespoons unsweetened shredded coconut

Directions – Caramel Sauce:
1. Puree the dates, vanilla powder, cinnamon, nutmeg, sea salt and allspice, along with the water in a blender or food processor.
2. If it seems too thick, add a little water one teaspoon at a time. The sauce should be thick but able to be piped and flow on the nachos later.
3. Pour the sauce into a recloseable plastic sandwich bag, seal it and set it aside.

Directions – Apple Base
1. Core and slice the apples, putting them in a bowl with the lemon juice to stop them from turning brown.
2. Arrange the apples on the bottom of a large plate. They can overlap a bit.

Directions - Toppings
3. The nut butter is an essential topping because it makes the dish sticky like cheese would. Place the nut butter in a recloseable plastic sandwich bag and seal it.
4. Cut off a corner of the bottom of this bag and pipe the nut butter onto the apples. I usually follow a crisscross pattern over the apples.
5. Add two or three of the other toppings and then cut a corner off the caramel sauce bag and pipe it onto the apple nachos. Serve immediately.

The next chapter will give you some the ingredients you will need to prepare the recipes that have appeared earlier in this book. While many of the items in this chapter can be purchased already pre-made (such as the ranch dressing and the hummus), you can ensure you're eating plant-based ingredients (and not strange chemical toxins) by making your own. Also, they'll save you some money when you make them yourself.

Chapter 11: Recipe Components

The following recipes are things you may need to make the other recipes in this book. I have included some pie and pizza crusts. There is also the applesauce that is my staple for sweetness and moisture to dishes. To add flavor to your foods, I include instruction for making your own vanilla extract, hot sauce, tomato sauce, salsa, Worcestershire sauce, soy sauce and more.

It'll help you to at least peruse this chapter so you know what's available. Making it yourself ensures that you have the purest ingredients for your recipes.

Almond Flaxseed Pie Crust

This crust is great for any pie in which you need a pre-baked crust. It also works when you are making a pie that calls for the crust to be baked with the filling. If it requires a top crust, just double the recipe. This crust is simple to make; it has only five ingredients and it comes out great every time.

Ingredients:
    2 tablespoons ground flaxseed
    5 tablespoons room temperature water
    1 cup almond flour, ground finely (if you can't find fine flour, put it in the blender and pulse a few times)
    ⅓ cup tapioca starch (sometimes called tapioca flour)
    ½ teaspoon salt

Directions:
1. Place the flaxseed and water in a bowl and stir to mix. Let it sit for 10 minutes.
2. In a large bowl, combine the almond flour, tapioca starch and salt. Add the flaxseed and water mixture and mix with a fork or use a pie cutter to form a dough that is damp but not sticky. If it's sticky, add more almond flour.
3. Shape the dough into a ball and place it in the middle of a sheet of parchment paper. Place another sheet of parchment paper on top and roll it flat, using a rolling pin.

4. Peel off the top layer of parchment paper and flip the crust over into a pie dish. Remove the top parchment paper and press dough into the edges and up the sides.
5. Prick the bottom and sides with a fork.
6. Put the crust in the freezer for about 15 minutes while preheating the oven to 400 degrees, Fahrenheit.
7. If you're making the empty crust, cover with foil and place pie weights or beans on top. Bake for 15 minutes. Uncover and cook for another 10 minutes, then retrieve it from the oven and let the crust cool to room temperature. Do not fill the pie until the crust is completely cool.
8. If you're baking the crust with the filling included, place the filling in the pie and cover it with a top crust if necessary. Bake as indicated by the pie recipe.

Applesauce

You Can Make Applesauce Chunky Or Smooth

Applesauce is highly versatile. You can use it as a side dish or a dessert. You can make it chunky or smooth. If you're using applesauce in a recipe, you'll most likely want it smooth and without flavorings, so it won't compete with the other spices.

I sometimes use a little sweetener when I make applesauce, because the apples I use are not particularly sweet. I prefer Empires, Granny Smiths, or Macintosh apples because they hold up to heat well and they provide a tart presence. The sweetener I use is either agave syrup or Stevia. Whatever you use, you'll want to taste the sauce before adding any sweetener; you may find you don't need any. This recipe makes two cups of applesauce.

Ingredients:
4 apples, peeled, cored and chopped into ½-inch pieces
½ teaspoon lemon juice
¾ cup water
1 pinch of sea salt
1 teaspoon agave nectar or half an individual packet of stevia
½ teaspoon cinnamon (optional)

Directions:
1. Place apples, lemon juice, water and salt in a saucepan over medium heat and bring it to a boil. Boil for 15 to 20 minutes, until the apples are soft when pierced with a fork.
2. Use an immersion blender to smooth. This is where you would add the sweetener and cinnamon, if desired. You can also use a potato masher to create a chunky consistency or just put it into a blender if you do not have an immersion blender.

Four Flour Options

Bleached flour is high in gluten; it is highly refined and therefore not the best for our continued good health. Here are four different flour options that can be used instead of the traditional white flour.

Oat Flour

Oat flour is the one I use most frequently, but fortunately for me, it is the easiest to make of the four. One cup of old-fashioned rolled oats will often make just a little less than one cup of oat flour. It depends on the recipe you are making, but you may want to hold out some whole oats and add them into the oat flour to add some bulk to the mix.

Ingredients:
1 cup old-fashioned rolled oats

Directions:
1. Place the oats in a food processor and pulse until they are ground to a powder (30 to 60 seconds)
2. Add the whole oats and whisk in by hand, if desired.
3. Store in an airtight container if you are not using it right away.

Chickpea Flour

Chickpea Flour Is Easy To Make In A High-speed Blender

Dried chickpeas can be ground into a flour that works well in many recipes. You do need a high powered blender because the chickpeas are pretty hard. It is probably best to have a high powered blender anyhow, since most other flours require the high speed. One cup of dried chickpeas will usually produce a little less than one cup of flour, I like to store the results of my grinding in the freezer to keep it fresh longer.

Ingredients:
1 cup dried chickpeas

Directions:
1. Place the chickpeas in the blender and turn it on low. Gradually increase the power until it reaches the maximum speed. Stop when the chickpeas have been ground as finely as possible.
2. Sift the flour into a bowl through a fine mesh sieve and place any pieces that are too large to pass back in the blender to be processed again. You may need to repeat this process two or three times before everything is ground to your satisfaction.

Brown Rice Flour

Brown rice flour is a little more complicated to make. You need a blender that is specifically designed to crack grains.

Ingredients:
4 cups rice

Directions:
1. Place the rice in the blender, one cup at a time.
2. Blend until you get it as fine as possible. (It will never be completely fine)
3. Store in an airtight container. Rice flour tends to get moldy, so it is advisable to keep it in the freezer until it is needed.

Coconut Flour

Coconut Flour Is Made From The Pulp Of The Coconut

This recipe is easy but you do have to crack a coconut, pour out the milk and remove the pulp from the shell. That's not my idea of fun, but the flavor of this flour is super and I use it frequently. Coconut flour is very expensive to purchase; once you make it yourself you'll understand why. Two cups of pulp will yield only about one cup of flour.

Ingredients:
Coconut pulp

Directions:
1. Preheat the oven to 120 degrees, Fahrenheit or as low as it will go.
2. Cover a baking sheet with parchment paper and spread the coconut pulp over the paper.
3. Bake for 45 minutes. If your oven doesn't go down to 120 degrees, you must watch the pulp carefully so it won't burn. It will take less than 45 minutes. The pulp is done when it is totally dry.
4. Remove the baking sheet from the oven and let it cool for at least 10 minutes

5. Place the dried pulp in a high-speed blender and process for one to two minutes or until it becomes a fine flour.
6. Store in an airtight container.

Creamy Ranch Dressing

I have a friend who is lactose intolerant and most ranch dressing bothers her, but she loves this. Its dairy free and delicious, made from almonds and coconut milk. The taste is very close to the commercial ranch dressing, but it comes without all the annoying side-effects of lactose. This recipe keeps well if refrigerated, lasting for up to a week. It yields 12 servings.

Ingredients:
1 cup coconut milk
¾ cup raw unsalted cashews
1 tablespoon lemon juice
1 tablespoon parsley, dried
2 teaspoons dill, dried
1 teaspoon salt
2 teaspoons onion powder
1 teaspoon garlic powder
1 teaspoon minced garlic
1 tablespoon white vinegar
2 teaspoons horseradish
2 teaspoons liquid coconut aminos (found in a health food store)

Directions:
1. Place the coconut milk in a bowl, add the cashews and let them soak for 10 minutes. Remove the cashews with a slotted spoon and place them in a food processor.
2. Grind the nuts into a fine texture, somewhat like wet sand.
3. Add the coconut milk gradually, scraping down the sides frequently, until it attains the consistency of a smooth paste.
4. Add the lemon juice, parsley, dill, salt onion powder, garlic powder and garlic and blend until smooth.

5. Add the vinegar, horseradish and coconut aminos; blend well.

Green Curry Paste

You only need a blender to prepare this paste. You'll find it gives all kinds of dishes and sauces a little extra zing. The results are gluten free and vegan. The paste will last, frozen, for about a month and refrigerated in a covered jar for about 10 days. This recipe yields about 1½ cups of green curry paste.

Ingredients:

3 small green chilies, stems and seeds removed and chopped
1 green bell pepper, chopped
3 cloves garlic, chopped
2 stalks lemongrass, trimmed, and chopped
6 green onions, chopped
1/2 teaspoon coriander
1 teaspoon cumin
1 teaspoon ground ginger
1 teaspoon ground turmeric
½ teaspoon ground black pepper
½ teaspoon sea salt
3 tablespoons lemon juice
1 lime, zested and juiced
2 tablespoons avocado oil
1 tablespoon maple syrup

Directions:

1. Place the green chilies, green pepper, garlic, lemongrass and green onions in a blender and process until somewhat smooth. The lemongrass will take some time to break down. Periodically scrape down any accumulation on the sides. The mixture will look like a thick paste.
2. Add the coriander, cumin, ginger, turmeric, pepper and salt; blend until thoroughly combined.
3. Add the lemon juice, lime zest and juice, avocado oil and maple syrup; blend into a paste consistency.
4. Place in a container and use at will.

Hot Sauce

Hot sauce is as hot as the peppers you use. I don't like it all that hot so I use Jalapenos. Other good peppers to use are cayenne and Fresno. You can add a half or whole habanero to give it punch if you like. Always wear rubber gloves when you work with hot peppers or you can burn the skin on your hands. If you do get them on your skin, rinse it off with whole milk. Even 2% milk will help, if that's all you have. You do not need to remove the seeds from the peppers; just put them in the blender and it will crush them up. Often, the seeds are what gives the pepper its heat.

You can store your hot sauce in an airtight container in the refrigerator for a few weeks. It is also possible to freeze it and thaw before using.

Ingredients:
20 fresh hot peppers
1½ cups white vinegar
½ teaspoon salt
3 teaspoons garlic, minced

Directions:
1. Wearing gloves, wash the peppers, cut off the tops and slice in half lengthwise; set aside.
2. Place the vinegar in a saucepan and add the salt and garlic. Pour the peppers in and bring to a boil.
3. Reduce and simmer until the peppers have become soft, about 10 minutes.
4. Pour the contents of the saucepan into your blender and blend until it liquefies. If you are adding habanera or other hotter pepper, add it here. Do not cook it. Taste before you add more to see if your hot sauce really needs it, then add in small amounts and taste before adding any more.

Hummus

Pour A Little Olive Oil And Paprika On Top For A Delicious Snack

Hummus is a wonderful snack all by itself. However, in this book, there are several recipes that incorporate hummus into the ingredients. This plain hummus is great with wheat crackers or raw vegetables. The recipe yields about 1½ cups.

Ingredients:
¼ cup tahini sauce
¼ cup fresh lemon juice
2 tablespoons olive oil
2 cloves garlic, minced
½ teaspoon ground cumin
½ teaspoons salt
1 15-ounce can chickpeas, drained and rinsed
2 to 3 tablespoons water
1 Dash paprika

Directions:
1. Place the tahini and lemon juice in the bowl of a food processor and process on high for one minute. Scrape the bowl down and process for another 30 seconds.
2. Add the olive oil, garlic, cumin and salt and process for 30 seconds. Scrape the sides down and process for another 30 seconds.

3. Add half of the chickpeas and process for one minute, scraping down the sides partway through. Add rest of the chickpeas and process until smooth.
4. There is a chance the mixture will be too thick. In that case add one teaspoon of water at a time, up to 3 teaspoons, processing until the paste is smooth and creamy.
5. Sprinkle with paprika and store in the refrigerator until ready to serve.

Ketchup

One tablespoon is considered a serving of this delicious ketchup and the recipe makes two cups. I store this in a canning jar; it will keep in the refrigerator for about a month.

Ingredients:
2 cloves garlic, minced
1 small onion, chopped
1 cup tomato puree
¼ cup apple cider vinegar
⅛ teaspoon allspice
⅛ teaspoon ground cloves
4 drops stevia
2 tablespoons Swerve
1 teaspoon sea salt
1 pinch ground pepper
¼ cup water (approximately; vary to adjust the thickness to your liking)

Directions:
1. Peel and chop the garlic and onion and place them in a saucepan along with the rest of the ingredients, except for the water; bring it to a boil.
2. Reduce the heat to low and simmer for 10 minutes, adding water if it becomes too thick.
3. Place the contents of the pan in a blender or use an immersion blender to process until smooth.

4. Pour into a jar and let it cool before covering and storing in the refrigerator.

Marinara Sauce

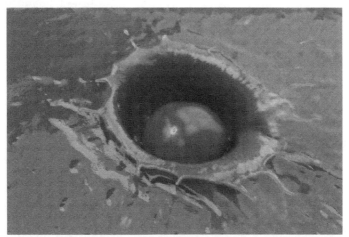

Blend Your Marinara Sauce Longer If You Like It Smooth

Marinara sauce is a little thinner than regular tomato sauce and it contains no meat. You can serve it over whole-wheat pasta, spaghetti squash, or anything else you want to give a touch of tomato flavor. I like to use Roma or plum tomatoes because they have a sweet flavor, but you can use any type of tomato. This recipe makes four cups of sauce.

Ingredients:
4.5 pounds fresh tomatoes, stems removed
2 tablespoons olive oil
5 cloves garlic, minced
½ cup onion, chopped fine
½ teaspoon salt
1 big sprig of basil with 4 to 5 leaves on it, leaves scored but not cut through

Directions:
1. Chop the tomatoes and put them in the bowl of a food processor. Pulse to break them down until the tomatoes look like salsa.

2. Pour the olive oil in a large skillet and heat it up.
3. Add the garlic and onion and sauté until the onion turns translucent.
4. Add the tomatoes and salt and sauté, bringing the mixture to a boil. Once it boils, turn down the heat to a simmer.
5. With a butter knife, score the leaves of the basil but do not cut all the way through. This will release the flavor. Set the sprig on top of the mixture in the skillet and press down with a spoon.
6. Simmer for 10 to 15 minutes and serve.

Mayonnaise – Vegan Style

I like this mayo because it is very tangy, thanks to the lemon juice and mustard. The recipe calls for prepared mustard but I suggest you try it with about a quarter teaspoon of ground mustard and see what you think. This recipe will make one small jar of mayonnaise. It must be refrigerated.

Ingredients:
1 teaspoon lemon juice
½ cup soy milk
1 cup canola oil
1 pinch salt
½ teaspoon prepared mustard

Directions:
1. Place the lemon juice and soy milk in a blender and process for 30 seconds.
2. While blending, slowly pour in the canola oil through the top of the blender so that the mixture thickens and emulsifies.
3. Add salt and mustard; blend to combine.
4. Pour into a sealable container and chill in the refrigerator before using.

Nut Butters

Make Nut Butters From Peanuts-Cashews-Almonds & Other Nuts

The following is a collection of nut butters that come in handy for cooking, but they are also good for eating on crackers or bread. I have included almond butter, cashew butter and peanut butter here and they are all made in a similar fashion. Always use raw nuts with no salt added. It is important that you roast the nuts or purchase them already roasted; otherwise you will not be able to get a creamy consistency. Each of these make a little more than one cup.

Almond Butter

Ingredients:
3 cups almonds
½ teaspoon sea salt

Directions:
1. Preheat the oven to 325 degrees, Fahrenheit and cover a shallow baking sheet with parchment paper or foil. Coat lightly with nonstick spray.
2. Spread the almonds out on the baking sheet in a single layer and bake for about six minutes.
3. Stir and bake for another six minutes or until golden.

4. Immediately place the hot almonds in a high speed blender. Let the blender run for about 10 minutes. Stop and scrape down the sides every five minutes or so. The nut butter should be smooth and creamy when done.
5. Place the butter in a glass jar and cover with a lid.

Refrigerate your nut butter and it will remain fresh for up to two months.

Cashew Nut Butter

I use roasted cashews for this recipe, but if you can't find them without salt, omit the sea salt from the recipe.

Ingredients:
2 cups roasted cashews
½ teaspoon sea salt

Directions:
1. Place the cashews in a food processer or high speed blender and process for 10 to 20 minutes or until the butter is creamy.
2. Add the salt and blend for 20 seconds.
3. Place in a glass jar and refrigerate. The butter will be good for two to three months.

Peanut Butter

I use dry roasted unsalted peanuts for this recipe and if you want you can roast your own as in the almond butter recipe above.

Ingredients:
2 cups peanuts
¼ to ½ teaspoon sea salt

Directions:
1. Place the peanuts in the high speed blender or food processor. Start on low speed to break down the peanuts

(they are a little harder than the other nuts). Process on high until it becomes smooth.
2. Add the salt and blend for 20 seconds.
3. Transfer to a jar and chill for eight hours before using to attain the correct thickness. It will be a little thin before going into the refrigerator.
4. This butter will last for up to six weeks in the refrigerator in a covered glass jar.

Plain Polenta

Polenta Is A Pretty Yellow Or White-Depending On The Cornmeal

Polenta is just cornmeal and water or milk that is used to add bulk to meals. An Italian friend of mine used to make polenta and mix in some cooked sausage and vegetables. She would pour it into a casserole dish and let it set. Then she cut it in cake-like squares, heated it up and poured marinara sauce on top with some cheese. I use a combination of water and plant-based milk because it makes the polenta a little bit creamier and adds some flavor. You can also use almond, soy, cashew or even coconut milk. This recipe makes four to five servings of polenta.

Ingredients:
4 cups water
1 cup plant-based milk
1½ cups cornmeal

¾ teaspoon salt

Directions:
1. Bring the water and milk to boil over medium heat and add the cornmeal.
2. Stir often until the mixture thickens.
3. Season with salt and serve.

Pumpkin Puree

Sure, you can go pick up a can of pumpkin puree at the grocery store, but do you know what is in that can along with the pumpkin? You may not want to put its preservatives and other stuff in your body. It is very easy to make your own pumpkin puree and you can freeze it for use later. The process is a little messy, but it is worth it because the taste is so much better.

Ingredients:
A small pumpkin
Water

Directions:
1. Remove the stem from the pumpkin and cut it in half.
2. Scrape out all the seeds with a spoon and reserve them to toast later.
3. Place the pumpkin, cut side down, on a baking sheet (or two) that has been covered with foil. Use a baking sheet with sides because you will be adding water.
4. Pour about a half inch of water into the pan.
5. Bake in a preheated 350-degree, Fahrenheit oven for 50 minutes or until you can pierce through the skin and flesh with a knife and then have little to no resistance.
6. Remove from the oven and let cool for less than an hour before refrigerating. Pumpkin can be a source of food poisoning; it grows pathogens quickly.
7. Once it is cool, scrape the flesh from the skin and transfer it to a bowl. Use an immersion blender or place chunks in a regular blender and blend until smooth.

8. Put in freezer bags and place in the refrigerator to cool completely if it isn't already cool. As soon as it is completely cool, you can store it in the freezer.
9. If you are using in the next day or two, you can refrigerate your pumpkin in a covered dish and it'll be fine. You can keep pumpkin in the freezer for up to four weeks. Because of the danger of harmful bacteria you'll want to thaw your pumpkin in the refrigerator, not on the counter. After four weeks, the puree will become too watery to use.

Refried Beans

Use Refried Beans As A Dip Or In Tacos Or Other Mexican Dishes

Refried beans make a great side dish and are often used to make tacos, tostados, burritos and other Mexican dishes. This recipe gives you four side servings.

Ingredients:
1 tablespoon olive oil
½ cup onion, finely chopped

2 cloves garlic, minced
¼ teaspoon sea salt
¼ teaspoon ground cumin
½ teaspoon chili powder
2 15-ounce cans pinto beans, rinsed and drained
½ cup water
2 tablespoons fresh cilantro, chopped
1 tablespoon lime juice

Directions:

1. Place a medium sized saucepan on the stove over medium high heat and pour in the olive oil allowing it to heat up.
2. Add the onions and sauté for three to five minutes.
3. Add the garlic and sauté for two to three minutes
4. Sprinkle in the salt, cumin and chili powder and stir for about 30 seconds.
5. Pour in the beans and water. Stir, cover and simmer for about five minutes.
6. Take a potato masher and mash the beans in the saucepan.
7. Simmer for another three minutes; remove from heat.
8. Stir in the cilantro and the lime juice.

Salsa

Delicious Salsa

This salsa has just the right flavor and heat. You'll want to wear kitchen gloves when you slice the jalapenos and remove the seeds; otherwise you may chemically burn your hands, as well as spreading it to other sensitive skin. If you prefer less heat, only use one jalapeno. This recipe makes about two cups of salsa.

Ingredients:
  1 small red onion
  2 cloves garlic
  3 large tomatoes
  1 to 2 jalapeno peppers
  ½ cup fresh cilantro
  3 tablespoons lime juice
  ¼ teaspoon sea salt or to taste

Directions:
  1. Peel and dice the red onion and place it in a bowl.
  2. Peel the garlic and mince it, placing it in the same bowl.
  3. Stem the tomatoes and cut them in half. Dice the tomatoes into small pieces and add to the bowl.
  4. Open the jalapenos and remove the seeds. Mince the peppers and add to the bowl.
  5. Chop the cilantro and put it in the bowl.
  6. Squeeze in the lime juice and sprinkle with salt. Stir and taste the results, adjusting the seasoning as needed.
  7. Store in a glass jar in the refrigerator.

Soy Sauce

This Soy Sauce Doesn't Have Any Soybeans, Yet It Tastes Great

Amazingly, soy sauce is easy to make and it is cheaper than buying at the store. The flavor of homemade soy sauce is superior to the stuff you get in the store. I store mine in pint mason jars in the refrigerator.

Ingredients:
¼ cup balsamic vinegar
¼ cup vegetable broth
1 tablespoon molasses
1½ cup water
¼ teaspoon garlic powder
¼ teaspoon ground ginger
⅛ teaspoon fresh ground pepper

Directions:
1. Pour the vinegar, broth, molasses and water in a medium saucepan and whisk it together. Turn the heat on to medium high.
2. Add the garlic powder, ginger and pepper and whisk everything together.

3. When the mixture starts to boil, turn the heat down to a simmer and let it cook for 20 minutes or until the liquid has reduced to about a cup.
4. Pour the liquid into a glass jar and let it cool before putting on the cover and placing it in the refrigerator.
5. Shake each time before using.

Tofu Basil Pesto

I love pesto sauce, but in order to make it creamy, you have to use parmesan cheese. This version switches out the parmesan cheese and replaces it with tofu making it completely plant-based. The recipe makes one cup of pesto that can be used in other recipes or over pasta. There isn't even any oil in this recipe.

Ingredients:
½ package extra-firm silken tofu (6 ounces or so), drained and dried
2 packed cups basil leaves
4 cloves garlic, chopped
2 teaspoons lemon juice
¼ cup toasted pine nuts or almonds
Sea salt to taste

Directions:
1. Drain and dry the tofu and cut it in chunks. Place it in the bowl of a food processor.
2. Add the basil leaves and garlic and pulse to break everything up.
3. Pour in the lemon juice, nuts and salt and process on high until the mixture is smooth and creamy.

Tomatoes, Diced

Ingredients:
6 vine ripened tomatoes (you can use more if you like, I just had six on hand)
½ tsp sea salt

285

Directions:
1. Wash and core the tomatoes.
2. Bring a large saucepan to a boil.
3. Drop the tomatoes in the water. Leave them there for one minute, then drain the water and toss them into an ice water bath to cool them down. It'll take about a minute.
4. Once the tomatoes are cooled, you can easily peel off the skins.
5. After the skins are gone, dice the tomatoes.
6. Put the diced tomatoes back in the saucepan with the salt and any other seasonings you may want to add. Let them simmer for about five minutes.
7. Remove and store, preferably in a glass jar, in the refrigerator. You can freeze them as well. Just use a freezer-safe container.
8. This recipe makes about two cups diced tomatoes. That is equal to a 15-ounce can of diced tomatoes.

Tomato Sauce

Ingredients:
5 pounds tomatoes
¾ teaspoon salt
2 tablespoons olive oil
1 tablespoon tomato paste (See recipe, Chapter 11.)
1 garlic clove, halved
1 basil sprig
1 bay leaf

Directions:
1. Cut the tomatoes in half horizontally. Squeeze out the seeds and discard them. Press the cut side of the tomatoes against the large holes of a box grater and grate tomato flesh into a bowl. Discard the skins. You should have about four cups of pulp and juice.
2. Put your pulp and juice in a shallow saucepan over high heat. Add the salt, olive oil, tomato paste, garlic, basil and bay leaf. Bring to a boil, then reduce the heat to a brisk simmer.

3. Reduce the sauce by almost half, stirring occasionally. This should produce about 2½ cups of medium-thick sauce. This will take 10 to 15 minutes. Adjust the salt to taste. It will keep for up to five days in the refrigerator; it also freezes well.
4. You should have about 2½ cups of tomato sauce.

Tomato Paste

Makes 20 to 24 ounces

Ingredients:
10 pounds tomatoes (See Recipe Note)
2 tablespoons olive oil
2 teaspoons sea salt
½ teaspoon citric acid

Directions:
1. Preheat the oven to 350 degrees, Fahrenheit.
2. Quarter the tomatoes.
3. Combine the tomatoes and olive oil in a large saucepan. Bring to a simmer. Cook until the tomatoes are soft and the peels begin to detach from the flesh.
4. Push the warm tomatoes through a food mill, sieve or chinois to separate the tomato pulp from the seeds and skins.
5. Stir the sea salt and citric acid into the pulp. Discard the seeds and skins.
6. Divide the tomato pulp between two large, rimmed baking sheets.
7. Bake the tomato pulp until it is reduced to a paste. Check the tomatoes every half hour, stirring the paste and switching the position of the baking sheets so that they reduce evenly. Over time, the paste will start to reduce to the point where it doesn't fill the baking sheet any more. At this point, combine the contents of the two pans into one and continue to bake.
8. The paste is done when it's shiny and brick-colored It will have reduced by more than half (3 to four hours). There

shouldn't be any remaining water or moisture separating from the paste at this point
9. Divide the finished paste into 4-ounce jars, leaving three quarters of an inch of headspace.

Plant-based Vanilla Extract

Inside The Vanilla Bean Are Black Seeds that Give the Flavor

Making your own vanilla takes a little time, but it is very easy and much cheaper than store-bought vanilla. You just need vodka and a vanilla bean. I soak the mixture until it turns dark, like vanilla ought to be; that takes about a month.

Ingredients:
1 fresh vanilla bean
½ cup of vodka

Directions:
1. Split the bean lengthwise and scrape out the vanilla seeds on both sides.
2. Place the seeds into a lidded pint sized glass jar, along with the vanilla bean pod.
3. Pour the vodka on top and close the lid.
4. Place the jar in a dark area and shake it two to three times a day for two weeks.

5. Shake the jar once a day for two to three more weeks or until the mixture takes on a dark brown color.
6. Store the jar in a dark, dry area and use at will.

Vegan Graham Cracker Crust

Graham Cracker Crusts Can Be Baked, Filled, Then Refrigerated

This crust is perfect for vegan cheesecakes and peach or apple pie. It is very easy to make using coconut oil and maple syrup along with crushed graham crackers. It makes one crust.

Ingredients:
1½ cup graham crackers, crushed (about 10 sheets)
3 tablespoons maple or agave syrup
3 tablespoons canola or coconut oil (Melt the coconut oil if it's not liquid already.)

Directions:
1. Combine the crushed graham crackers, maple or agave syrup and canola or melted coconut oil in a bowl and stir with a wooden spoon until well combined.
2. Press into a 9-inch pie pan and bake in a preheated 350 degree, Fahrenheit oven for eight to 10 minutes or until the surface turns golden brown. Let the crust cool to room temperature before filling.

Vegetable Stock

A nice canned vegetable stock is hard to come by, so I always concoct my own. It isn't very difficult to make and the taste is superior by far to what you will find commercially made.

When I make vegetable stock, I don't peel anything. The carrot peels and onion peels go right in because you are just going to strain them out anyway. Plus it gives the stock more flavor and definitely more nutrients.

When finished, your vegetable stock can be frozen and, as with all these stocks, it will last for up to four months in the freezer. This recipe makes four to five quarts depending on how long you simmer it.

Ingredients:
    2 onions, not peeled but quartered
    4 celery stocks with leaves attached, cut into two-inch pieces
    3 carrots, not peeled, but cut into one-inch pieces
    5 sprigs fresh thyme
    1 small bunch fresh parsley
    1 bay leaf
    1 teaspoon whole peppercorns
    6 quarts water

Directions:
1. Place all the ingredients into a stock pot. Cover with water and place over high heat until it starts to simmer. When it starts to bubble around the edges, reduce the heat to low.
2. Cover and simmer for one hour without stirring.
3. After the hour is up, give it a stir to circulate the vegetables. Simmer for one to two hours on very low heat, stirring every 15 minutes.
4. Strain through cheesecloth and cool to room temperature before placing your stock the refrigerator or freezer.

Whole Wheat Pizza Dough

Anything Goes With A Whole Wheat Pizza Crust

This pizza dough is crispy and delicious. It does contain yeast, which will need 18 to 24 hours to rise, so I mix mine up the day before I want to use it. This recipe will give you three thick pizza crusts or six thin ones.

Ingredients:
   1 teaspoon active dry yeast
   7 cups whole-wheat flour
   1 to 4 teaspoons of salt to your taste
   3 cups water, with more if the dough seems dry

Directions:
1. Place the yeast and flour in a mixing bowl and set up the mixer with a dough hook. Turn it on low to mix the yeast and flour together.
2. Gradually add the water while mixing. Knead with the hook for two minutes or until the dough starts to form in a ball. If you need more water, add it.

3. Grease a clean bowl and place the dough in. Cover with plastic wrap and place it in a warm area to rise for 18 to 24 hours.
4. Turn out onto a floured board and shape in a long oval. Cut six or three sections. Fold the ends of each section toward the middle, flip the dough and shape it into a ball.
5. Place parchment paper on a baking sheet and set the dough balls on the baking sheet. Cover with a clean towel and let it rise for an hour.
6. If you do not want to cook all the dough immediately, put some of the balls in a freezer bag and stash them in the freezer. When you're ready to use one, let it defrost then proceed by setting the ball on the parchment-covered baking sheet and continue with the recipe.
7. Roll or push the dough out into a circle, top with sauce and veggies and bake.

Worcestershire Sauce

Make your own Worcestershire Sauce with spices and herbs and you won't believe the flavor. This recipe makes ⅔ cup, just put it in a jar and keep it in the refrigerator. If you can find unfiltered apple cider vinegar, it makes the sauce a little more potent. You'll find coconut aminos at your local health food store.

Ingredients:
½ cup apple cider vinegar
2 tablespoons coconut aminos
2 tablespoons water
¼ teaspoon onion powder
¼ teaspoon garlic powder
¼ teaspoon ground mustard
¼ teaspoon ground ginger
⅛ teaspoon ground cinnamon
⅛ teaspoon ground black pepper

Directions:
1. Whisk together the vinegar, coconut aminos and the water in a small saucepan.

2. Add the onion powder, garlic powder, mustard, ginger, cinnamon and black pepper and whisk together.
3. Turn the fire to medium heat and bring to a low boil. Reduce the heat and simmer for two minutes.
4. Cool, pour into a small jar with a lid and refrigerate.

Chapter 12: Yummy Recipes For Your Cravings

Sometimes you just want a plain old pizza, hamburger or hot dog. You miss chicken nuggets, tacos or macaroni and cheese. Sometimes you just want something sweet and crunchy for fun. This chapter will let you indulge without too much guilt. Here you will find plant-based recipe for faux hotdogs, hamburgers, tacos, chicken nuggets and even some sweet flavored popcorns that will keep you happy and healthy. Please do remember that although the popcorn recipes do not have refined sugar in them and they are sweet and still have calories, so limit your consumption.

Almond Vanilla Popcorn

Crunchy And Delicious Almond Vanilla Popcorn

When I was a kid, my family used to rent a cabin up by "the lake," which was a summer community with cute little shops and restaurants that were only open during the summer months. One of the store fronts was owned by a lady who sold all kinds of flavored popcorn. Since then, I have always loved flavored popcorn and have collected tons of recipes for them. Unfortunately, however, most of them include refined sugars. I have worked to discover several ways to make flavored popcorn work when using other sweeteners. This is what I came up with. It uses dates for sweetness.

You can pop the popcorn however you would like. I have even used microwave popcorn. This recipe makes 16 cups of popped popcorn, but if you keep it in an airtight container, it will keep for about a week before turning stale.

Ingredients:
½ cup popcorn kernels
2 Medjool dates
2 tablespoons coconut oil
2 tablespoons slivered almonds
2 teaspoons vanilla (See recipe, Chapter 11.)
1 tablespoon water

Directions:
1. Preheat the oven to 325 degrees, Fahrenheit and prepare casserole dishes or baking sheets with parchment paper.
2. Pop the popcorn and place in a large bowl.
3. Combine the dates, coconut, almonds, vanilla and water in a food processor and process until smooth, scraping down the sides a few times.
4. Pour the sauce into the popcorn and mix to be sure it is all well coated.
5. Spread the popcorn out on the parchment paper, it will be wet, so you'll need baking sheets with shallow sides.
6. Place the popcorn in the oven and bake for eight to 10 minutes, stirring with a wooden spoon every two minutes. The popcorn is ready when it is dry.
7. Cool and store in an airtight container.

Carrot Hotdogs with Red Cabbage

This is a fun recipe that uses carrots instead of hot dogs. The carrots are marinated overnight and then you make the cabbage slaw that goes with them. Kids don't often like the slaw, but they do like the carrot dogs. This makes four carrot hot dogs.

Ingredients:
4 carrots, each about the size of a hot dog
¼ cup tamari sauce
1 tablespoon maple syrup
¼ cup water
1 tablespoon liquid smoke
1 teaspoon garlic powder
1 tablespoon paprika (sweet variety)
2 tablespoons nutritional yeast (optional)
3 tablespoons olive oil
1 small onion, sliced
2 apples, peeled, cored and cut into slices
2 more tablespoons maple syrup
1 small head red cabbage
2 tablespoons apple cider vinegar
Salt and pepper to taste
1 more cup water
1 more tablespoon olive oil
4 whole-grain hot dog buns
Ketchup and mustard (See recipe for ketchup, Chapter 11.)

Directions:
1. Boil the carrots for 12 to 14 minutes or until tender, in enough salt water to cover them. Drain and set the carrots aside to cool.
2. Combine the tamari, a tablespoon of maple syrup, the water, liquid smoke, garlic powder, paprika and nutritional yeast in a shallow dish. Add the carrots after they are cool, cover them and place them in the refrigerator for 24 hours to marinate.
3. Make the red cabbage slaw by heating the three tablespoons of olive oil in a Dutch oven and adding the onion. Sauté until translucent.

4. Add the apple slices and the remaining two tablespoons of maple syrup, then sauté for four to five minutes until the apples are tender
5. Cut the cabbage into strips and combine them with the apple cider vinegar in another pot on the stove. Stir, cover and simmer for about 10 minutes.
6. Add the salt and pepper to taste with the water. Stir and simmer for 30 minutes. Drain out any leftover liquid.
7. Place the final tablespoon of olive oil in a skillet over medium heat and fry the carrots on all sides, cooking them for two to three minutes on each side.
8. Slice the buns, add a little cabbage slaw and a carrot and serve with ketchup and mustard.

Chickpea Burgers

Savory And Delicious Chickpea Burgers

These burgers don't taste like regular ground beef patties, but they do have a flavor all their own and it is delightful. This recipe requires you to cook them in a skillet. I've tried to grill them, but it didn't work very well. They require the infusion of skillet oil to become crispy and to gain the right flavor and texture. The recipe makes six to eight burgers.

Ingredients:

1 15-ounce can chickpeas, rinsed and drained well
½ cup green onions, finely chopped
⅓ cup fresh dill, finely chopped
2 tablespoons dry whole-wheat breadcrumbs
2 tablespoons lemon juice
½ teaspoon salt
¼ teaspoon pepper
¼ teaspoon ground cumin
2 tablespoons tahini
¼ cup vegetable oil

Directions:
1. Pour have the chickpeas in a bowl and mash with a potato masher.
2. Add the green onions, dill, bread crumbs and lemon juice and mix well.
3. Place the rest of the chickpeas in a food processor and add the salt, pepper, cumin and tahini. Process until smooth.
4. Add to the mashed chickpeas in the bowl and mix well, using your hands. Shape them into six to eight patties.
5. Heat up a 12-inch skillet over medium heat and pour in the vegetable oil. Let it heat up, then add the patties and cook them until crispy and dark golden on both sides, for about six minutes. Only flip them once.
6. Drain on paper towels and serve alone or in buns with condiments.

Chickpea Crust Pizza With Veggie Topping

I don't think it is a secret that I like to cook with chickpeas. I love the flavor they lend to dishes. Also most chickpea dishes are easy to make. This one is no different. The crust pizza crust is made from chickpeas and the topping is a vegetable topping, but you can use just about topping you like. The marinara sauce and the chickpea flour used in this recipe can both be found in Chapter 11. This makes one pizza.

Ingredients:
1 cup chickpea flour

1 cup unsweetened soy milk
1 tablespoon apple cider vinegar
1 tablespoon tahini
¼ teaspoon baking powder
¼ teaspoon sea salt
⅛ teaspoon ground pepper
1 zucchini, diced
1 red bell pepper, seeds removed and diced
½ cup cauliflower florets, chopped
1 cup marinara sauce
¼ teaspoon crushed red pepper flakes

Directions:

1. Pour the chickpea flour, soy milk, apple cider vinegar, tahini, baking powder, salt and pepper into a blender and blend into a smooth batter.
2. Coat a skillet with nonstick spray and cook the batter over medium heat for 20 minutes. Keep the heat down so it doesn't burn. Use a wide spatula to flip the crust over and cook for another 10 minutes. Transfer to a cooling rack. Cool completely before topping.
3. Preheat the oven to 350 degrees, Fahrenheit and line a baking sheet with parchment paper. Make the topping.
4. Spray another skillet with butter flavored nonstick spray and sauté the zucchini, bell pepper and cauliflower for five to seven minutes until tender crisp. Add a little water if they start to burn or stick.
5. Top the crust with marinara sauce and spread the topping over it.
6. Bake for 10 to 15 minutes or until the marinara starts to bubble.

Dark Chocolate Hazelnut Popcorn

Your Friends Will Love These, Packaged In Gift Bags

I make this and give it as gifts during the holiday season. Just put some in a festive goodie bag and tie it shut. This treat is good to have around any time you have guests. I place it in bowls to enjoy as an after-dinner treat with tea or coffee. The recipe makes five servings.

Ingredients:

    3 tablespoons coconut oil, divided
    ¼ cup unpopped popcorn kernels
    2 tablespoons cocoa powder
    ½ cup unsweetened coconut flakes
    ½ cup chopped hazelnuts
    2 tablespoons maple syrup
    ¼ teaspoon kosher salt

Directions:

1. Place two tablespoons of the coconut oil in a large pot with a lid.
2. Add the popcorn kernels, heat, shake and allow them to pop.
3. Once all the corn has popped, remove the pan from the heat and stir in the cocoa powder, coconut, hazelnuts, maple syrup and salt.
4. Mix well so that all the popcorn is coated; spread the kernels out on a baking sheet until they are dry.
5. Store at room temperature in an airtight container.

Greek Pizza

When I think of Greek cuisine, I think of olives and hummus along with goat cheese. Goat cheese isn't plant-based, but sometimes I do put some on my Greek pizza! Use any of the crusts in this book, but I like the whole-wheat one best (See Chapter 11). This makes one pizza.

Ingredients:
½ to 1 cup hummus, depending on how thick you like it. (See recipe, Chapter 11.)
1 handful sliced Kalamata olives
½ red pepper, seeded and sliced in strips
½ small red onion, diced
8 to 10 fresh basil leaves

Directions:
1. Preheat the oven to 375 degrees, Fahrenheit.
2. Spread hummus on the crust to about a half inch from the edge.
3. Sprinkle on the olives, red pepper and onion evenly over the surface of the pizza.
4. Place the basil leaves evenly on the pizza.
5. Put in the oven and cook for about 20 minutes (this is without a precooked crust). Check after 15 minutes and the pizza is done when the crust turns a light golden brown and the vegetables are cooked through.

Mexican Pizza

Try A Tasty Mexican Pizza

This is another great pizza recipe fit for lunch. Instead of tomato sauce, you use refried beans. You'll find the recipe for that later on in this chapter. This is a pizza version of a taco without the lettuce (there is spinach though). Use the chickpea crust found in Chapter 11 and change out the veggie toppings and marinara for the ingredients that follow.

Ingredients:
½ to 1 cup refried beans (depending on size of crust) (See recipe, Chapter 11.)
½ package mild taco seasoning
½ cup salsa
½ small yellow onion, diced
1 handful sliced black olives
1 tomato, stemmed and thinly sliced
1 handful fresh spinach leaves
¼ cup fresh cilantro, chopped

Directions:
1. Preheat the oven to 375 degrees, Fahrenheit.

2. In a small bowl, mix the cold refried beans with the taco seasoning and spread over the pizza crust to within a half inch of the edge.
3. Spread the salsa on top (use more if you want).
4. Sprinkle the onion and olives over the surface of the pizza.
5. Place the thin slices of tomato over the surface of the pizza and top with spinach leaves and cilantro.
6. Cook for 15 to 20 minutes or until crust is crispy and the vegetables are soft. The refried beans and salsa should be bubbly hot too.

Cinnamon Roll Popcorn

More popcorn? I couldn't help myself because this one is good and you don't use refined sugar to make it. Coconut palm sugar is usually found in a health or whole food store. This recipe calls for maple syrup, but if you do not want a maple flavor (I think it goes well with cinnamon) you can find coconut nectar at a health food store. This will allow the cinnamon flavor to come through even better.

Ingredients:
2 teaspoons vegetable oil
⅓ cup popcorn kernels
2 tablespoons coconut palm sugar
½ teaspoon ground cinnamon
2 tablespoons vegan butter
1 tablespoon maple syrup

Directions:
1. Use the vegetable oil in a large pan with a lid to make the popcorn according to package instructions.
2. Once the popcorn is popped, place the coconut palm sugar, cinnamon, butter and maple syrup in a saucepan over medium high heat. Stir constantly until everything melts and is well combined.
3. Place the popcorn in a large bowl and drizzle the sauce over the top. Toss with two large spoons to combine and let it cool before serving.

4. Store it at room temperature in an airtight container.

Pumpkin Flavored Popcorn

Serve Your Pumpkin Popcorn In A Pumpkin

Those of you who salivate when pumpkin spice coffee comes out in early September will also appreciate this popcorn treat. It uses pumpkin puree and you can find out how to make your own in chapter 11 of this book. It makes about 10 cups of popped corn and you will want to devour it all at one time.

Ingredients:
10 cups popped popcorn (about ⅓ cup kernels)
2 tablespoons maple syrup
2 tablespoons coconut oil, melted
1 tablespoon pumpkin puree
¼ teaspoon cinnamon
½ teaspoon salt

Directions:
1. Make the popcorn and place it in a large bowl, reserving two cups of the popcorn to be placed in a four-cup measuring cup.
2. Preheat the oven to 325 degrees, Fahrenheit.

3. In a small saucepan, combine the maple syrup, coconut oil, puree, cinnamon and salt and put over medium heat. Stir constantly while it cooks, for about two minutes.
4. Put all the popcorn except the reserved two cups into a large roasting pan lined with aluminum foil.
5. Pour the sauce over the popcorn in the roasting pan and stir until it is all coated.
6. Place in the oven for eight minutes, stirring every two or three minutes.
7. Remove from oven and let it cool; the popcorn will harden.
8. Pour the two cups of plain popcorn on top and stir to break up the hardened popcorn and incorporate all together.
9. Store at room temperature in an airtight container.

Quinoa Tacos

Use any color quinoa you like, but I usually use the red quinoa because it looks more like meat. Use your own vegetable broth and salsa found in chapter 11 or just use store bought types. This makes six servings.

Ingredients:
1 cup quinoa
¾ cup water
1 cup vegetable broth
1 tablespoon nutritional yeast
½ cup salsa
½ teaspoon garlic powder
2 teaspoons chili powder
2 teaspoon cumin
½ teaspoon sea salt
½ teaspoon ground pepper
1 tablespoon olive oil

Directions:
1. Rinse the quinoa and drain.

2. Heat a saucepan over medium heat and toast the quinoa for about four minutes stirring constantly.
3. Add the water and vegetable broth and bring to a boil.
4. Reduce to a simmer, cover and cook for 15 to 20 minutes or until the liquid is all absorbed. Fluff with a fork, put the lid back on and set to cool 10 minutes.
5. Preheat the oven to 375 degrees, Fahrenheit and cover a shallow sided baking sheet with aluminum foil.
6. Place the cooled quinoa in a mixing bowl and add the nutritional yeast, salsa, garlic powder, chili powder, cumin, salt, pepper and oil and stir to combine.
7. Spread on prepared baking sheet and bake 20 minutes, stir around in the pan and bake another 15 or 20 minutes or until it starts to smell good and becomes light brown.
8. Serve in taco shells or on tostadas.

Sweet Potato Burgers With Maple Flavor

You Can Top A Sweet Potato Burger Just Like A Hamburger

These burgers are made with sweet potatoes and a grain called millet. They taste sweet and spicy and you may even prefer them over a hamburger. This recipe makes four servings.

Ingredients:
1 large sweet potato, peeled, cubed and steamed until tender (about two cups)
¾ cup water
¼ cup dry millet
2 dates, pitted
1 cup baby portobello mushrooms, quartered
2 teaspoons cilantro
1 chipotle pepper
1 teaspoon cumin
½ teaspoon kosher salt
1 lime, juiced
1 tablespoon maple syrup
¼ cup Old fashioned rolled oats
1 tablespoon pumpkin seeds
Canola oil

Directions:
1. Attach the "S" blade in the food processor and add in the sweet potato cubes.
2. In a saucepan, place the water and bring it to a boil. Add the millet, cover the pot and simmer for 15 minutes or until all the liquid is absorbed. Let the millet cool.
3. Place the dates, mushrooms, cilantro, chipotle pepper, cumin and salt in the food processor and process until everything is well diced and still chunky.
4. Preheat the oven to 350 degrees, Fahrenheit and cover a shallow-edged baking sheet with foil.
5. Place the sweet potato mixture in a large bowl and add the millet.
6. Add the lime juice, maple syrup, oats and seeds and mix with your hands. Divide into four portions and form patties.
7. In a skillet, heat up about a tablespoon of canola oil and place one patty in and fry until both sides brown. Place on the prepared baking sheets. Do the same with the other three patties adding more canola oil if necessary.

8. Place the baking sheet in the oven for 10 minutes.
9. Serve the patties on a bun with lettuce and condiments.

Sweet Potato Macaroni and Cheese

Whole Wheat Pasta Is Much More Nutritious Than Plain Pasta

This creamy sweet potato goodness is simply wonderful. You may not ever want the regular kind ever again. This makes six servings and it will go fast. Use it as a main dish for lunch and no one will skip it.

Ingredients:
1 14-ounce package whole grain macaroni
1 large (12 ounces) sweet potato, peeled and chopped
1 cup onion, chopped
½ teaspoon dried rosemary, crushed
½ teaspoon grated nutmeg
2 cloves garlic, minced
¼ teaspoon sea salt
¼ teaspoon ground pepper

Directions:

1. Preheat the oven to 425 degrees, Fahrenheit and coat the inside of a two-quart casserole with nonstick spray.
2. Cook the macaroni per package instructions, drain it and dump it into a large bowl.
3. In a medium saucepan over medium heat cook the sweet potato in enough salted water to cover it. Boil for 15 to 20 minutes or until the potato is tender. Drain off the water.
4. In a blender process the drained sweet potato and onion until chunky.
5. Add the milk and process until smooth and creamy, scraping down the sides as necessary.
6. Add the rosemary, nutmeg, garlic, salt and pepper and process until smooth.
7. Pour the sauce over the cooked macaroni and stir well. Pour into the prepared casserole and bake for 15 to 20 minutes or until brown and bubbly.

Tofu Hot Dogs

Tofu tastes however you want it to, by adding the flavors you want. I have a problem sometimes with the texture. Surprisingly enough, tofu is the perfect base for faux hotdogs because of its texture. You can boil them, fry them in a skillet, or grill them. I suggest grilling them, because they take on a more of a normal "hot dog" color. The tofu dogs will need to marinate overnight. This recipe makes eight tofu hot dogs.

Ingredients:

8 ounces firm tofu, drained and dried with paper towels
3 tablespoons olive oil
¼ cup water
2 tablespoons tamari sauce
1 teaspoon onion powder
1 teaspoon garlic powder
1 teaspoon coriander
1 teaspoon dry mustard
1 tablespoon paprika, smoked
½ teaspoon ground cardamom

¼ teaspoon allspice
1 cup vital wheat gluten (found at health food stores)
1 teaspoon granulated or powder sweetener of your choice
1 teaspoon salt
½ teaspoon ground pepper
⅔ cup oat flour (See recipe, Chapter 11)
1 teaspoon cornstarch or arrowroot powder
Whole wheat buns and condiments

Directions:
1. Preheat the oven to 350 degrees, Fahrenheit.
2. Crumble the tofu into a food processor and add the olive oil, water and tamari. Blend until smooth.
3. Add the onion powder, garlic powder, coriander, dry mustard, paprika, cardamom, allspice, wheat gluten, sweetener, salt, pepper, oat flour and cornstarch; process until smooth.
4. Remove the ball of dough from the food processor and knead it with your hands for about two minutes. Divide it into eight equal portions.
5. Shape each portion like a hot dog and wrap it in a piece of aluminum foil, twisting the ends. Place them seam side down in a baking dish.
6. Pour about a half inch of water into the bottom of the dish and bake for one hour.
7. Let it cool a little and carefully unwrap each tofu dog. (Watch out for steam!)
8. Place on a plate and cover with plastic wrap, storing it in refrigerator overnight.
9. Simmer in hot water, fry in a skillet, or cook on the grill and serve on buns with condiments.

Vegan Caramel Popcorn

Add Liquid Organic Food Coloring For More Fun

Caramel corn was always a treat for me. I either got it when we went to the movie theater or at the county fair.

This recipe is almost as good as the original. It makes eight cups. Just keep in mind that it does contain brown sugar. I tried making it with date sugar and it came out good, but with a unique, flavor. This makes eight cups of caramel corn.

Ingredients:
8 cups popped popcorn
½ cup vegan butter
⅔ cups brown sugar
2 tablespoons agave nectar
¼ teaspoon baking soda
1 pinch salt
1 teaspoon vanilla (See recipe, Chapter 11.)

Directions:
1. Preheat the oven to 250 degrees, Fahrenheit and line a baking sheet with parchment paper.
2. Spread the popped popcorn on the baking sheet and set it aside.
3. In a saucepan, over medium heat, melt the butter.

4. Add the brown sugar and whisk constantly until it starts to bubble.
5. Add the agave nectar, baking soda, salt and vanilla and stir. Because of the baking soda it will foam quite a bit; just keep stirring until the foam goes down.
6. Once the foaming stops, pour it onto the popcorn and use a spatula to turn the popcorn while drizzling in a stream. Make sure all the corn is coated and pat smooth with the spatula.
7. Bake for one hour, stirring it up every 15 minutes. You're done when the popcorn is crispy.

Zucchini Nuggets

Try Some Zucchini Nuggets To Tame Your Garden

Use these as a substitute for chicken nuggets or make them a little smaller and use them like tater tots. They have a lovely texture and flavor. I serve them with ketchup, barbeque sauce, or ranch dressing. (You'll find these recipes in Chapter 11) This recipe makes about 20 to 30 nuggets (2 tablespoons each).

Ingredients:
6 to 7 small potatoes, peeled and cut into quarters
2 medium zucchinis, grate
½ teaspoon sweet paprika
¼ teaspoon salt

¼ teaspoon ground pepper
Olive oil

Directions:
1. Cook the potatoes in boiling water until they are tender when poked with a fork. Drain and let them cool so they can be handled.
2. Preheat the oven to 425 degrees, Fahrenheit and line two baking sheets with parchment paper. It is hard to get them all on one baking sheet, but the second may only be half full.
3. Grate the zucchini and squeeze out the liquid by wrapping it in a clean kitchen towel and twisting and squeezing. Place in a medium bowl.
4. Grate the cooked potatoes and place them in the bowl with the zucchini.
5. Add the paprika, salt and pepper, adjusting to your taste and mix with your hands.
6. Scoop out 1½ to two tablespoons of the mixture at a time and shape them into nuggets or tot shapes. Brush each one with olive oil on all sides. Place on baking sheets.
7. Bake for 35 to 40 minutes or until they are crisp.

Now you are ready to start your plant-based diet. You have an arsenal of recipes and are on your way to more vibrant health.

Conclusion

You are now well on your way to eating great while fueling your body with the healthy nutrients needed to live a productive and energy charged life! The 200 recipes in this book are all plant-based and delicious. Here, we've covered your whole day, from the time you wake up to midnight snacks. You now have at your disposal everything you need to get started on the path towards a healthier way of living. By reducing or eliminating meat from your diet, you can not only feel better, but you can be confident that you are fueling yourself, family and friends with delicious meals that can bring vibrant health.

Now it's time to begin frequenting the produce section of your local grocery store – if you haven't already. It will make you healthier in the long run and will enable you to live a more energy filled life. Revisit the first couple chapters of this book to refresh your memory on which foods are the most helpful to you in your pursuit of great plant-based meals. Swap out one unhealthy food item each week that you *know* is not helping you and put in its place one of the plant-based ingredients that you like. Then have some fun creating the many different recipes in this book. Find out what recipes you like the most so you can make them often and most of all; have some fun exploring all your recipe options.

I wish you great health and delicious meals on your life's journey!

Thanks for reading.

If this book has helped you or someone you know then I invite you to leave a nice review right now. ***It would be greatly appreciated!***

My Other Books

For more great books simply visit my author page or type my name into the search bar: **Susan Hollister**

Author Page

USA: https://www.amazon.com/author/susanhollister

UK: http://amzn.to/2qiEzA9

Thanks and Enjoy!

Made in the USA
Lexington, KY
02 May 2019